The Year of the Poet XI

March 2024

The Poetry Posse

inner child press, ltd.

The Poetry Posse 2024

Gail Weston Shazor
Shareef Abdur Rasheed
Teresa E. Gallion
hülya n. yılmaz
Noreen Snyder
Tzemin Ition Tsai
Elizabeth Esguerra Castillo
Jackie Davis Allen
Mutawaf Shaheed
Caroline 'Ceri' Nazareno
Ashok K. Bhargava
Alicja Maria Kuberska
Swapna Behera
Albert 'Infinite' Carrasco
Michelle Joan Barulich
Eliza Segiet
William S. Peters, Sr.

In order to maintain each poet's authentic voice, this volume has not undergone the scrutiny of editing. Please take time to indulge each contributor for their own creativity and aspirations to convey their uniqueness.

hülya n. yılmaz, Ph.D.
Director of Editing ~
Inner Child Press International

General Information

The Year of the Poet XI
March 2024 Edition

The Poetry Posse

1st Edition : 2024

This Publishing is protected under Copyright Law as a "Collection". All rights for all submissions are retained by the Individual Author and or Artist. No part of this Publishing may be Reproduced, Transferred in any manner without the prior **WRITTEN CONSENT** of the "Material Owners" or its Representative Inner Child Press. Any such violation infringes upon the Creative and Intellectual Property of the Owner pursuant to International and Federal Copyright Laws. Any queries pertaining to this "Collection" should be addressed to Publisher of Record.

Publisher Information
1st Edition : Inner Child Press
intouch@innerchildpress.com
www.innerchildpress.com

Copyright © 2024 : The Poetry Posse

ISBN-13 : 978-1-961498-19-8 (inner child press, ltd.)

$ 12.99

WHAT WOULD
LIFE
BE WITHOUT
A LITTLE
POETRY?

Dedication

This Book is dedicated to

Humanity, Peace & Poetry

the Power of the Pen

can effectuate change!

&

The Poetry Posse

past, present & future,

our Patrons and Readers &

the Spirit of our Everlasting Muse

*In the darkness of my life
I heard the music
I danced...
and the Light appeared
and I dance*

Janet P. Caldwell

Table of Contents

Foreword — *ix*

Preface — *xiii*

Renowned Poets — *xv*
   Nâzim Hikmet

The Poetry Posse

Gail Weston Shazor	1
Alicja Maria Kuberska	9
Jackie Davis Allen	15
Tezmin Ition Tsai	23
Shareef Abdur – Rasheed	29
Noreen Snyder	35
Elizabeth Esguerra Castillo	41
Mutawaf Shaheed	47
hülya n. yılmaz	55
Teresa E. Gallion	61
Ashok K. Bhargava	67
Caroline Nazareno-Gabis	73

Table of Contents . . . *continued*

Swapna Behera	79
Albert Carassco	85
Michelle Joan Barulich	91
Eliza Segiet	97
William S. Peters, Sr.	103

March's Featured Poets — 111

Francesco Favetta

Jagjit Singh Zandu

Carmela Núñez Yukimura Peruana

Michael Lee Johnson

Inner Child Press News — 139

Other Anthological Works — 177

Foreword

Renowned Poets

Nazım Hikmet

The March 2024 issue of our international monthly book, *The Year of the Poet, has* its focus on the Turkish modernist poet, playwright, novelist, screenwriter, director, memoirist and activist Nazım Hikmet.

As a native from Turkey—born, raised and schooled there, who independently studied the books of this "Blue-Eyed Giant" after the ban on them was lifted in 1965, I assert that his life and works demand voluminous analyses . . . a task that cannot be completed within the constraints of this text. Being acutely aware of the challenge at hand, I shall resort to your understanding for the brevity of my words. A few factual glimpses on the personal and literary phenomenon that the name *Nazım Hikmet* embodies will have to suffice. One three-step-fact remains unchanged; namely, that Nazım is universally acknowledged as Turkey's exceptional modern poet but also as a world poet, and has exhausted—continues to exhaust—the research venues of countless minds at home as well as abroad.

Nazım Hikmet was born in 1902 as Mehmet Nazım Ran in Selânik and raised in Istanbul. When Turkey was occupied by her allies after World War I, he left for the Soviet Union [sic]. His higher education included his degree in Economics and Sociology at the Communist University of the Toilers of the East in Moscow. It is there where Russian Futurists and Symbolists, writers and visual artists, as well as Lenin's ideology influenced him. When the Turkish War of Independence resulted in the establishment of the Republic of Turkey in 1924, Hikmet returned to Turkey.

Soon after his return to his beloved motherland Turkey, Nazım started working for *Aydınlık*, a liberal newspaper. Having stigmatized his person and his work as "Communist", the Turkish state banned his poems. In addition, he was sentenced to 15 years in prison for sedition but fled to the Soviet Union, returning to Turkey in 1928 and settling in İstanbul. There, he worked at various newspapers and magazines and film studios, published his first poetry books and wrote his plays (1928-1932).

In 1938, Nazım Hikmet was charged as a "traitor" for the crime of inciting the Turkish armed forces to revolt. He was sentenced to 28 years and 4 months in prison. After serving approximately 11 years of his sentence, an international campaign fought for his release. A committee that included Pablo Picasso, Paul Robeson, and Jean-Paul Sartre was formed in 1949, and in the spring of 1950, Hikmet began a hunger strike in protest of the Turkish Parliament for its failure to include an amnesty law in its agenda before it closed for the upcoming general election. He was freed under the forgiveness law of 1950 at last.

As the recorded numbers and facts of history reveal, much of Nazım Hikmet's life was spent behind prison walls: 17 years in Turkish prisons and another 12 years in exile. After his death of a heart attack in Moscow in 1963, his works continued to be banned in Turkey until 1965. Multiple decades after his death, highly justified celebrations are being conducted around the world for this "Blue-Eyed Giant", as Nazım Hikmet became to be known posthumously. Knowing now that he knew to say "I lived", it seems only appropriate for us to conclude our brief visit with his own celebratory words:

My Funeral

Will my funeral start in our courtyard below?
How will you bring my coffin down three floors?
The lift will not take it
and the stairs are too narrow.
Perhaps the courtyard will be knee-deep in
sunlight and pigeons
perhaps there will be snow and children's cries
mingling in the air
or the asphalt glistening with rain
and the dustbins littering the place as usual.
If in keeping with the custom here I am to go, face
open to the skies,
on the hearse, a pigeon might drop something on
my brow, for luck.
Whether a band turns up or no, children will come

near me,
children like funerals.
Our kitchen window will stare after me as I go,
the washing on the balcony will wave to see me off.
I have been happier here than you can ever imagine,
friends, I wish you all a long and happy life.

hülya n. yılmaz, Ph.D.

Professor Emerita (Liberal Arts), Penn State, U.S.A.
Director of Editing Services at
Inner Child Press International, U.S.A.

Coming April 2024

www.innerchildpress.com/world-healing-world-peace-poetry

Coming May 2024

www.innerchildpress.com/now-open-4-submission

Preface

We, **Inner Child Press International, The Year of the Poet** and **The Poetry Posse** welcome you.

WOW ... a decade. We are so excited as we have now crossed over into our 11th year of **The Year of the Poet**.

This particular year we have chosen to feature renowned poets of history. We do hope you enjoy. Read ~ Learn.

For those of you who are not familiar with our story, back in 2013, a few of us poets got together with the simple intention of producing a book a month. That was our challenge. Since that time the enterprise has blossomed and brought forth a fruit that seems to keep on growing as evidenced as we enter 2023.

Our purpose is simple. Through our lyrical words and verse, we not only wish to share our poetic works, but we also have the poetic naiveté to believe that we can assist in the growth of consciousness of the things that have an effect our collective humanity. Therefore, we welcome your readership. For more about what we are attempting to accomplish, have a look at our Publishing Web Site ... www.innerchildpress.com. If you would like to know a bit more about this particular endeavor please stop by for a visit at :

www.innerchildpress.com/the-year-of-the-poet

Over the years, Inner Child Press has been socially active to bring awareness and catalog through literature the things that have an impact upon our world and its inhabitants. We have solicited, produced, underwritten and published quite a few volumes to that end. For more insight you may wish to visit : www.innerchildpress.com/the-anthology-market. If you are a writer, poet, or activist, you would be advised to keep a eye out for upcoming volumes should you desire to participate. All readers are welcomed as well. Note, that there is a myriad of published volumes that are available as a FREE PDF download as well as available for purchase at affordable prices.

We at this time extend to you our well wishes for your own personal journey and hope that you consider including us as a travel companion.

Bless Up

Bill

William S. Peters, Sr.

Publisher
Inner Child Press International
www.innerchildpress.com

Renowned Poets
Nâzim Hikmet

March 2024

by hülya n. yılmaz, Ph.D.

Let's say we're seriously ill, need surgery—
which is to say we might not get up
                from the white table.
Even though it's impossible not to feel sad
                about going a little too soon,
we'll still laugh at the jokes being told,
we'll look out the window to see if it's raining,
or still wait anxiously
                for the latest newscast . . .

    ~ From: Nazım Hikmet, "On Living, II"

"On Living" by Nazım Hikmet is traced back to 1948, during which the author was imprisoned for his revolutionary activities in the political arena. Divided in three parts, the poem embodies Hikmet's philosophical illustration of living a simple life. His motivating call for hope and love accentuates the kind of living that materializes entirely in the present. His conceptualization of *being* rather than *doing* shines throughout this renowned poetic construct. The following quote from the first part of the same poem puts all doubts at ease when Nazım's intent is concerned:

Living is no laughing matter:
       you must live with great seriousness
             like a squirrel, for example—
  I mean without looking for something beyond and above living,
         I mean living must be your whole occupation.

The more closely we read, the more convinced we become why "On Living" is situated on a high pedestal of literary platforms worldwide. Composing his words with down-to-earth diction, Hikmet stands by his readers interactively, not alienating them through exclusionary contexts. His lines quoted below from part I speak for themselves:

I mean, you must take living so seriously
    that even at seventy, for example, you'll plant olive trees—
    and not for your children, either,
    but because although you fear death you don't believe it,
    because living, I mean, weighs heavier.

The reason as to why Nazım Hikmet was imprisoned by a regime that stood on shaky grounds for its fear of socio-political changes seems to rise above the surface in the ensuing sections (from part I and II respectively):

Living is no laughing matter:
    you must take it seriously,
    so much so and to such a degree
  that, for example, your hands tied behind your back,
                  your back to the wall,
  or else in a laboratory
    in your white coat and safety glasses,
    you can die for people—
even for people whose faces you've never seen,

> even though you know living
> > is the most real, the most beautiful thing.

{}   {}   {}

> Let's say we're at the front—
> > for something worth fighting for, say.
>
> There, in the first offensive, on that very day,
> > we might fall on our face, dead.
>
> We'll know this with a curious anger,
> > but we'll still worry ourselves to death
> > about the outcome of the war, which could last years.
>
> Let's say we're in prison
> and close to fifty,
> and we have eighteen more years, say,
> > > before the iron doors will open.
>
> We'll still live with the outside,
> with its people and animals, struggle and wind—
> > > I mean with the outside beyond the walls.
>
> I mean, however and wherever we are,
> > we must live as if we will never die.

"The Blue-Eyed Giant", as Nazım Hikmet was called posthumously in a most affectionate manner by countless people across the globe, concludes his 3-part poem "On Living" with a call for hope and love within the framework of *being*, as mentioned in this text initially:

> This earth will grow cold,
> a star among stars
> > and one of the smallest,

a gilded mote on blue velvet—
        I mean *this*, our great earth.
This earth will grow cold one day,
not like a block of ice
or a dead cloud even
but like an empty walnut it will roll along
        in pitch-black space . . .
You must grieve for this right now
—you have to feel this sorrow now—
for the world must be loved this much
        if you're going to say "I lived".
. .

How many of us are presently in a position "to say 'I lived' . . ."? Are we constantly doing rather than *being*? Any seventy-year-olds among us? Do they/Do we have the motivation "to plant olive trees", even though we do not expect them to be ready for our own children?

In Nazım Hikmet's words, when will it be time for us to *live* "without looking for something beyond and above living", *living* being our "whole occupation"?

hülya n. yılmaz, Ph.D.

Professor Emerita (Liberal Arts), Penn State, U.S.A.
Director of Editing Services at
Inner Child Press International, U.S.A.

*Poets . . .
sowing seeds in the
Conscious Garden of Life,
that those who have yet to come
may enjoy the Flowers.*

Poets, Writers . . . know that we are the enchanting magicians that nourishes the seeds of dreams and thoughts . . . it is our words that entice the hearts and minds of others to believe there is something grand about the possibilities that life has to offer and our words tease it forth into action . . . for you are the Poet, the Writer to whom the Gift of Words has been entrusted . . .

~ wsp

Poetry succeeds where instruction fails.

~ wsp

Now Available

www.innerchildpress.com/the-anthology-market.com

Open for Submissions

www.innerchildpress.com/now-open-4-submission

Gail Weston Shazor

Gail Weston Shazor

Gail Weston Shazor is a lover of words. She is fond of the arcane, unusual and the not yet words.

Coining words at an early age, there was often a bit of trouble with teachers, but she always had her mother and aunt to back up her choices in expression. Born in Mississippi, she spent her early years with her grandparents. Each of the four left very careful influences on her pre-schooling. She learned in turn how women worked in and out of the home and how men worked in and out of the home to support the family. She learned that a lack of proper schooling was not the only way to learn and understanding life was a great teacher. As in most rural families of color, women had a greater chance of formal learning. Both of Gail's grandmothers read out loud to the family whether it was the bible or the newspapers and important documents to their spouses.

Gail Weston Shazor has authored (so far) Notes from the Blue Roof, A Overstanding of an Imperfect Love, HeartSongs and Lies My Grandfather's Told Me. The number of anthologies is too many to list with the premier accomplishment of one of the contributors to The Year of The Poet. Gail will always lend her ink to community projects and will purchase the books of fellow poets in the Inner Child Press family.

Mizz Ma'am

I wish that I were a raving beauty
The kind of woman
That men strand straighter
To pass by
Suck in their stomachs
Adjust comb-overs
And wish for years that have passed
Them by

I wish that I were a raving beauty
Platinum haired and stilletoed
Chestnut brown with locks to my waist
Wearing a dress that drapes across
Curves that long to be touched
Needily
The invitation apparent to eyes that see
With blinders

I wish that I were a raving beauty
With bad habits
Chain smoking and swearing and whiskey
That you must excuse
Because
I am me afterall
And these are things you expect
In a devil may care woman

I wish I were a raving beauty
And yet
I know you find comfort in the fact
That I am not that kind of woman
A beauty of legendary proportions
So instead
I will make changes in other's lives
By continuing to just rave…

Poets...Double Etheree

I
Always
Find wonder
In the graces
Of a shared spirit
Your voices speak to me
Even when I cannot hear
Above the ringing in my ears
Or the tiredness that holds my soul
This can never be an average story
Each of our tales is individual
And unique in the passion we show
Whether we are still in love's thrall
Or on the edge of fragileness
We share life with each other
Through the nib of our pens
And I am so blessed
To each of you
I can say
You are
Friends

No regrets

Today I am wonderful
Where yesterday I was not
I have lived in between time
Where minutes and hours
Hold no sway to the moon
Golden seconds shining
With no true reflection
For even dust needs light
In order to be seen by the eye

Today I am wonderful
For last week I was not
My heart seat was askew
And beating irregularly in my chest
Pressing the tears upward
Through my throat and lungs
Into ducts unwilling to shed them
For fear that they will never stop

Today I am wonderful
As my yesterdays have been
When covered by your wings
Beating the time on the wind
Matching my breath to yours
To bring me up higher than you
Though our blood's origin is the same
As you are in my heart, I will always be

Alicja Maria Kuberska

Alicja Maria Kuberska

Alicja Maria Kuberska – awarded Polish poetess, novelist, journalist, editor.

She is a member of the Polish Writers Associations in Warsaw, Poland and IWA Bogdani, Albania. She is also a member of directors' board of Soflay Literature Foundation, Our Poetry Archive (India) and Cultural Ambassador for Poland (Inner Child Press, USA)

Her poems have been published in numerous anthologies and magazines in : Poland, Czech Republic, Slovakia, Hungary,Ukraina, Belgium, Bulgaria, Albania, Spain, the UK, Italy, the USA, Canada, the UK, Argentina, Chile, Peru, Israel, Turkey, India, Uzbekistan, South Korea, Taiwan, China, Australia, South Africa, Zambia, Nigeria

She received two medals - the Nosside UNESCO Competition in Italy (2015) and European Academy of Science Arts and Letters in France (2017). Ahe also received a reward of international literary competition in Italy „ Tra le parole e 'elfinito" (2018). She was announced a poet of the 2017 year by Soflay Literature Foundation (2018).She also received : Bolesław Prus Prize Poland (2019), Culture Animator Poland (2019) and first prize Premio Internazionale di Poesia Poseidonia- Paestrum Italy (2019).

Nâzım Hikmet Ran Borzęcki
Citizen of the World

Turkey's unruly son,
born in Greece,
adopted by Poland,
found refuge in Russia,
and Bulgaria sang
loudly with his voice

No one and nothing can stop the power of words
which unfurled their wings and flew into the world,
to spread communist slogans and fight for freedom.
On their way they stopped for a moment
to rest on an enamoured cloud
and dance the legend of love in the ballet

The poems broke through the prison walls
They described
the human landscapes of homeland
and discovered
the meaning of the word "romanticism",
later they asked the passers-by
 - Do you still cry on buses?

Today

I conquer another day
I read the titles of articles
and I know
that infinitives screaming loudly now
tomorrow will lose their voice,
their meaning.

The words
"everything and everyone",
puffed up with pride today,
are doomed to pass away.
They will leave without a trace,
without a second thought.

Events - these imprudent ones,
will leave a couple of anecdotes,
a smile in memories,
a few feathers on the pavement

Trace

Love occurs in spring
in pastel colours.
In the city park
the first tulips have bloomed.

Life awakens again
and appearances of death vanish
- they dry up like puddles
born by winter thaws

The sun's rays swathe / cover the earth,
for hope to be reborn,
and from distant lands
the birds and dreams have returned.

Wrinkles

I try to outsmart fate
and I pretend
that old age does not exist.
I twist myself like an old coat,
I pay tribute to eternal youth.

The mirror laughs mockingly
at clumsy tricks.
It shows my silver hair
and dull eye shine.

And time... strolls on the skin
like a drunk hen in the snow.
It leaves dark spots
and chaotic paw prints.

Jackie
Davis
Allen

Jackie Davis Allen, otherwise known as Jacqueline D. Allen or Jackie Allen, grew up in the Cumberland Mountains of Appalachia. As the next eldest daughter of a coal miner father and a stay at home mother, she was the first in her family to attend and graduate from college. Her siblings, in their own right, are accomplished, though she is the only one, to date, that has discovered the gift of writing.

Graduating from Radford University, with a Bachelor's of Science degree in Early Education, she taught in both public and private schools. For over a decade she taught private art classes to children both in her home and at a local Art and Framing Shop where she also sold her original soft sculptured Victorian dolls and original christening gowns.

She resides in northern Virginia with her husband, taking much needed get-aways to their mountain home near the Blue Ridge Mountains, a place that evokes memories of days spent growing up in the Appalachian Mountains.

A lover of hats, she has worn many. Following marriage to her college sweetheart, and as wife, mother, grandmother, teacher, tutor, artist, writer, poet and crafter, she is a lover of art and antiques, surrounding herself, always, with books, seeking to learn more.

In 2015 she authored *Looking for Rainbows, Poetry, Prose and Art*, and in 2017, *Dark Side of the Moon*. Both books of mostly narrative poetry were published by Inner Child Press and were edited by hulya n. yilmaz in 2019, *No Illusions. Through the Looking Glass*, which was nominated to be considered for a Pulitzer Prize by the publisher and editor of Inner Child Press, ltd.

http://www.innerchildpress.com/jackie-davis-allen.php
jackiedavisallen.com

An Uncommon Man

A poet, man of letters, screenwriter.
Librettist, theorist, director of films,
Nazim Hickmet was a committed Communist.

A writer of free verse,
His nationality was dispossessed.

Rejected for his political views.
His verse was disallowed, banned.
Punished for his vision.

Unwavering, Nazim Hickmet
Was imprisoned for many years.

He died in Moscow, in exile, his heart broken.
Not in Turkey, his homeland. Was buried
In the Soviet Union. Not his choice.

A man of many and varied talents, the poet,
Hickmet won the International Peace Prize.

Sarah's Candle

Carrying grief heavier than winter's coat,
Sarah's mother wandered as her mind paced the floor.
So great the loss, her mind strayed everywhere.
And Sarah, she hid her light and tried not to weep.

The vigil began just as soon as the lifeless body
Had been laid out, prepared, sanitized with alcohol.
Stifling copious tears, Sarah solemnly stared
At the funeral strips of soiled and stained cotton.

A ritual for things without life, no longer breathing.
Match sticks, for want of pennies place marked
The site of baby's eyes. Death had snatched the light
From the day, so Sarah peeked around a wall of legs.

Female giants, the familiar kind: Momma, auntie, Grammy.
The tails of their aprons, tangled, yet starched bright.
Like a picture in a frame, the tiny body mute.
The muslin gown, newly made.

The pine-board box, cold and rough, hand hewn
From pain and splintered, from her father's reserve,
Replaced baby's potential for words, tears, love.
The name of life was gone. Grief ruled the day.

Erie mourning wails mingled
With echos of ghostly laughter, some singing.
Little more than a toddler, she feared death.
It comes to all, she was told. At the wake.

Sarah guessed it was true.

Black Ice

It was a bold, blustery Sunday morning,
A sickly shade of red painted the sky.
A ferocious winter storm was brewing.

Dark clouds hungrily fed her dread.

Echos of crashing waves, much like cymbals,
Drowned not the reason for her disbelief.
The grieved one prayed steadfastly:

That love might be treasured. That it be returned.

Evening availed itself of its persistent hue,
Like the insistence of her abiding faith.
The flame of her bedside-candle flickered.

The window-pane framed its reflection.

Fear's face stained, sad, her looking glass.
With grief. What she saw there left her in shock.
Aghast! Was there a knock at the door?

Tzemin Ition Tsai

Tzemin Ition Tsai

Dr. Tzemin Ition Tsai comes from the Republic of China(Taiwan). In addition to being a professor of literature at a university, he is more committed to writing poems, novels, and proses. He is also an editor of "Reading, Writing and Teaching" academic text, an International editor of "Contemporary dialogues" literary periodical in Macedonia, and Vice-Chairman of the International Jury of the SAHITTO INTERNATIONAL AWARD in Bangladesh, and a columnist for "Chinese Language Monthly" in Taiwan.

In a wide range of literary creations, he is particularly fond of interesting stories or novels, and writing articles or poems about the feelings of nature and human beings. He has won many national literary awards. His literary works have been anthologized and published in books, journals, and newspapers in more than 55 countries and have been translated into more than 24 languages.

The Fall of Autumn

I often peek at your shop, to see.
You, carelessly sitting on the granary floor.
Your hair gently lifted by the dusty wind.
The furrow sleeps in the half-harvested.
Scent of poppies, and you.
With a bunch of flowers retained on your cuff, entwined.
Like a gleaner, steady not in the field.
An hour, and then another hour.
The sun, well-cooked, conspires on how to carry.
The last seeping blessing.
The season of abundant fruits, the vines around the thatched house.
Brimming with fruit.
Filled with a mature core, intending to make the hazelnut shell plump.
With the sweet taste of nuts bursting, to welcome more sprouting.
Until the warm days never cease.
Where is the song of autumn?
Only because, the mottled clouds bloom softly.
Rose-colored touch on the stubble plain.
With the breeze either born or extinguished.
The hillside now has a soft soprano.
The whistle emanating from the garden, the swallows chattering in the sky.

Lonely Solitude

In the night of silver light,
A lonely figure stands upright.
His heart, a silent minstrel in the endless night,
Like a hermit in a land out of sight.
The world cannot change the fleeting dance,
The whispering wind enhances the trance.
Stories of joy and sorrow, trapped in the shadow of the morrow,
He moves forward alone; his shadow is his only fellow.
In what seems to be an endless quest,
His eyes hide stories, once ablaze,
Now at rest, they are cold, untold,
Loneliness reflected, as deep as the ocean fold.
Unique tranquility,
That gives his restless heart a temporary unwind.
He strides forward alone, as a lone figure in the twilight,
Guided by the celestial bodies in the night.

So Haggard

Only to see the spring wind as usual, casually with the willows on the embankment.
The goslings are yellow when the sky is clear and bright.
The vermilion gate has not opened, and the small rain is drizzling in the sunny weather.
Having wasted a lifetime in haggardness, who knows how many dusks have passed?
The fallen red petals make the water in the pond level.
In the apricot garden, the cuckoo cries, helpless that spring has already returned.
Outside the willow, on the painted building, who is twirling the flower branches on the railing?
It's just speechless facing the slanting sunlight.
In the fragrance of the falling flowers and outside the wave shadows, one is self-satisfied with their talents.
Not surprised to see the clear dawn of the buildings when separated from the group, the curtains are dusk again.
In youth, there is no regret for the mistake of fame, knowing it's hard to meet when it's time to part.
Haggard, haggard, the candle burns out leaving only red tears.
The shallow pool and lotus pond leaves are dry, the fine wind makes the egret cold.
Last year's summer rain hooked the plate, the moving clouds crossed the river, and the duckweed stems only left behind.
A lone trace floating in the dream soul of the world.
At the beginning, I was startled and shy, and when we met again, I was haggard.
Now the songs and wines are all reduced, but my worries are endless.

Shareef Abdur Rasheed

Shareef Abdur Rasheed

Shareef Abdur-Rasheed, AKA Zakir Flo was born and raised in Brooklyn, New York. His education includes Brooklyn College, Suffolk County Community College and Makkah, Saudi Arabia. He is a Veteran of the Viet Nam era, where in 1969 he reverted to his now reverently embraced Islamic Faith. He is very active in the Islamic community and beyond with his teachings, activism and his humanity.

Shareef's spiritual expression comes through the persona of "Zakir Flo" . Zakir is Arabic for "To remind". Never silent, Shareef Abdur-Rasheed is always dropping science, love, consciousness and signs of the time in rhyme.

Shareef is the Patriarch of the Abdur-Rasheed Family with 9 Children (6 Sons and 3 Daughters) and 41 Grandchildren (24 Boys and 17 Girls).

For more information about Shareef, visit his personal FaceBook Page at :

https://www.facebook.com/shareef.abdurrasheed1
https://zakirflo.wordpress.com

Mehmed Nazim Ran

Born day: Jan. 15 1902
Return day: June 03, 1963
in Selanik, Ottoman Empire
creative genius free spirit,
gifted artistic free thinker
soaked in truth, expression,
influenced by brothers,
sisters long gone who did
not embrace status quo
who never adhered to
go along to get along
so, he bumped heads
with the rulers
so, he spent many years
in dungeons
locked away so that his
power in his pen would not
bust through the falsehood
to be exposed as truly
weak diseased by corruption
houses built on sand crumble
down when a true force come
through like level 5 hurricane
his mind was blessed
but rulers don't enjoy them
boat rocked
nothing new been going on
players names change
the same intense hunger
to ignite the masses
to demand truth, honesty,
trust for the people
by the people

artist of variety of genre
have encountered to
this moment that same
reality when they won't
compromise their heart
through their work
speak truth to power
actually, it's truth speaking
to yet another evil version
of fake temporary domination
Mehmed Nazim lived in a
era of worldwide turmoil
and his pen was the bomb

winds..,
----
swirl around gathering strength
defying logic, bent on making itself
felt, and felt it surely shall be
unmistakably,
upon degree
" Be and it shall be "
clearly risen
storm clouds on the horizon
as written down, revealed to
Muhammad *(saw)
**Nabi Allah by thee
one(1) lord of all the worlds
Allah^(swt)
^^Rabil alamin
earth will convulse
throw alarmin its contents
in full view
full force unleashed upon rebellious
mankind
dem who got the message and rejected
put the book behind their back
and continue to act adverse to the verse
went backwards in reverse
life can be a curse if one's spiritual ear is
deliberately deaf, eyes blind
for them darkness looms even when
sun shines
for them yoke remains around neck
head forced up because they would not
bow down in prostration the most humble
demonstration of submission
dem doomed to humiliation

most unfortunate condition
all because they thought this life was their paradise
failed to reflect, inspect, review the verse revealed in full view
so their so called paradise became
their curse.
*(saw) = peace be upon him
**Nabi Allah = prophet of Allah.
^(swt) = All glory to Allah.
^^Rabil alamin = lord of all the worlds included; mankind & Jinn

free fall..,

from grace
beginning of human race
continues till today
astonishing as it may seem
mankind obviously don't read
for certain took no heed
" if you do not learn from history
you're doomed to repeat "
the nerve of a sperm drop
developed into a clot
into a lump of flesh in that boat
that floats
did not read and take heed
to the first *wahi
" READ IN THE NAME OF YOUR
LORD THAT CREATED YOU FROM
A CLOT "
feed, sustained lived, thrived
without breathe
this womb could easily had been
a tomb
how could one not only survive
but thrive in the womb?
instead after 9 months head
protrudes
a human developed, grew
from grace, even removed waste
received mothers food
from something
like tube but called umbilical
such a miracle
yet soon became typical
that same human became vain

oblivious to what's actually obvious
pure wonderment of human
development
though as improbable as it would seem
became an open adversary
a penchant to rebel as the whispering
devil does his evil
he who whispers into the hearts
to tear souls apart
he who use what's gleaming
appears fair seeming
as it would not have been smart
to disconnect from that source of life
at the start
it remains the same to let the devil snatch
your heart
make you forget how you were begot from
the start
and forget him who not only created the
heart, holds control of all hearts and souls
devil is cold unlike the abode where he
and his followers will dwell
the epitome of hot... hell
*wahi = revelation

Noreen Snyder

Noreen Snyder

Noreen Ann Snyder has been writing since she was a teenager. She writes a variety of different topics. Her favorite poetic forms are Sonnets, Blitz, Haiku, Tanka, and Free Verse. She always learning different poetic forms.

Noreen Ann Snyder is a poet, writer, and an author of five books, (four books are co-authored with her late husband, Garry A. Snyder.) Her poetry is in several Inner Child Press Anthologies. She is the founder of The Poetry Club on Facebook.

Nazim Hikmet

Nazim Hikmet spent a lot of years in prison
for his political beliefs.
He was a Marxist.
He wrote about love, human experience, nature,
revolution, and patriotism.
He gave up on using the traditional forms and
wrote using free verse.
To this day, he is the most important and influential
poet in Turkish Literature
and one of the great international poets
of the 20th Century.
What we can learn from him
is to be our own person,
stand up for what we believe in
and not to be afraid.
No matter what other people say.

My Best Friend

As I was taking a walk,
I noticed a huge crowd over yonder,
I went over there to see
what was going on.
I just couldn't believe it's happening
to my best friend!
I saw those cruel men put
a crown of thorns
on His head 'til there was blood.
OH, MY GOD! OH, MY GOD!
Then (oh, my Jesus) they beat Jesus
with a leather strap 'til
you can see only bones sticking
out of His back.
OH, HOW AWFUL! OH, HOW TERRIVBLE!
How can those men be so cruel to Him!
I asked a stranger why they're doing this
and he said, "He's guilty."
GUILTY? BUT AN INNOCENT MAN!
HE'S MY BESTFRIEND.
Then I turned away from him
and looked up.
OH, MY GOD! They're nailing His wrists and ankles
to the cross.
STOP! STOP! HE'S AN INNOCENT MAN!
HE'S THE SON OF GOD!
I LOVE JESUS. HE'S MY BESTFRIEND
THE BESTFRIEND THAT I'VE EVER HAD.
DON'T DO THIS TO HIM!
DON'T YOU SEE HE'S INNOCENT!
OH, MY JESUS! YOU CAN'T BE DEAD!
I LOVE YOU! I LOVE YOU, JESUS!

Sobbing I walked away very slowly to my house
very lonely 'cause He's gone.
Three days later,
I awoke from a horrible nightmare,
then...then there I saw Him.
OH, JESUS! YOU ARE ALIVE!
OH, MY JESUS!
He spoke clearly, "I'm making a home
for you in Heaven.
When you die, you're going to be with me
for being so faithful to me.
I love you so much that I was willingly
to die on the cross for you.
But now I arose again."

The Reflection in the Mirror

When I look into the mirror,
I see the reflection of myself.
How do I see myself?
Am I pretty or ugly? Sexy or not?
Am I friendly and kind
or mean and cold-hear ted?
Am I smart or stupid?
Do I like myself or do I hate myself?
How do I feel about myself?
As I look into the mirror once again,
I smiled at the reflection
because I like myself for who I am.
It doesn't matter what others think of me.
I am happy and satisfied with myself.
I like myself! That's what counts!

Noreen Snyder

Elizabeth E. Castillo

Elizabeth Esguerra Castillo

Elizabeth Esguerra Castillo is a multi-awarded and an Internationally-Published Contemporary Author/Poet and a Professional Writer / Creative Writer / Feature Writer / Journalist / Travel Writer from the Philippines. She has 2 published books, "Seasons of Emotions" (UK) and "Inner Reflections of the Muse", (USA). Elizabeth is also a co-author to more than 60 international anthologies in the USA, Canada, UK, Romania, India. She is a Contributing Editor of Inner Child Magazine, USA and an Advisory Board Member of Reflection Magazine, an international literary magazine. She is a member of the American Authors Association (AAA) and PEN International.

Web links:

Facebook Fan Page

https://free.facebook.com/ElizabethEsguerraCastillo

Google Plus

https://plus.google.com/u/0/+ElizabethCastillo

A Writer of Hope

Nazim Hikmet, a modern Turkish poet,

Promotes optimism in his pieces

A writer of hope that our world needs

Hikmet, a nationalist patriot

His masterpieces went beyond borders and race

Made us aware of many things that we must face

According to him, "the most beautiful seas hasn't been crossed yet",

And so, we should not do things that we will later regret.

A New Genesis

In Genesis they held hands together,
A Paradise in unity, love abounds
The Tree of Life stood in their midst
Prohibited by God to get near to it.
Cast away, they walked to the ends of the Earth,
Reincarnated lives continue to haunt their souls
The Tower of Babel they built to reach the Heavens
But God forbade them and off they fell.
The Great Flood came, vanishing lives in an instant,
A New World emerged, a new age daring flight
The New Adam and Eve built an empire,
Worked hard to achieve whatever they desired.
The haunting of the past continues its saga,
Plagues kept testing the spirit of humankind
The parted Red Sea of blood was a catalyst,
In sending people to a new Promised Land.
But still man was discontented,
Money and riches were all on his mind
Greed over power to him was an adventure,
Until came the Day of Rapture.
Pandemics can alter the lives of many
But not all can experience the Epiphany,
What if all these only test our faith?
And that the dawning of a new Genesis is at hand?
Tomorrow we can witness a brand-new beginning,
Full of hope that we can all survive
That the weary will have confidence in himself,
And the sickness will be healed in time.

Be Amazed

wake up to a brand-new dawning day
the radiant rays of the sun smiling your way
blue skies awakening this desire in your heart
Embark on your mission, have a thrilling start.
be amazed at the wonders what this world can bring
creation of God can all be but stunning
let the soft whispers of the southern wind caress your weary soul
forget about the worries let your senses be enthralled!
this life could be at times harsh on you
but wait, don't fret, don't let yourself immerse on being blue
be amazed at a grandiose beauty in front of your eyes
sail on your wondrous journey, don't let yourself be capsized.
yes, at times travelling on this vast ocean can be turbulent
but stay put on your ground, don't go against the current
remain steadfast through the complexities this world throws at you
shout at the top of your lungs, God I'm amazed by You!

Mutawaf Shaheed

Mutawaf Shaheed

C. E. Shy has been writing since the seventh grade. He continued writing through high school, until he became more involved in sports. After his graduation, he worked at the White Motors Company where he wrote for the company's newspaper. He started a column called: "The Poet's Corner." That was his first published work.

www.innerchildpress.com/c-e-shy.php

In Between Hikmet

Wind born rhymes sometimes,
I hear them fresh from the seas
I sit by. In between the places that
have influenced me. Leveraging
these verbal treasures, so they
comfort me.

Mixed in my mind are the places
and times that kept me free. Under
the influence of so many scenes,
the waves on the water bring mess-
ages to me. Remembering the old
castle that still lingers by the sea.

Where ever I go the image lays
with my memory. Not able to count
the struggles that follow the one that
went before. Grandad told me stories
from the days of yore. Legacy after
legacy erases the culture wars.

Pen in hand I remain steadfast to the
last dot and dash. Searching for the
scraps of paper I threw in the trash,
some words that were written, I balled
up in my fist, now are lost to the void.

How can I un-block the bridges that lead to
humanity? Not able to keep the pace I must
escape to a place where I can remain the
same.

Personally

I had to reach inside my dream to redeem you.
I never figured out how you ever got there. For
real I didn't care. I had to hurry and take you
in hand I didn't care if the dream didn't under-
stand. You had never been that far away. The
dream tried to hold you. It kept offering me
things I knew weren't true. Tugging at my
imagination for it to expand and go after some-
thing that was impossible to imagine. I already
had that in you. At first it was going to hide
you in day dreams.

Then thought it could rebuff me by telling me
what love means. The dream switched from riding
a car to flying in the sky. It broke into many pieces
in order to confuse me. We struggled and tussled
from New York City, to the Chinese main land.
From the wind- blown snows to Egyptian sands.
It resorted to threats and stern demands. Using
scary sounds then offering thousands of grands.

Wake up, wake up, somehow thinking that would
interrupt my plans. Lady, I was out to get you! The
dream pulled some old monsters I met before, I
used to see them in the one- dollar store. It sent
another dream to inter the fray, it was the same one I
had the other day. I stopped to wonder why it was
so demanding on holding you so tight. I remembered
it was past midnight. That's what dreams do, that
late at night. It was all resolved when I heard the call,
my wife shook me and said , baby time to awake,
the adhan was just called, it was time to make salat.

The Measurements

On the grand scale of things how do I measure and weigh the losses and gains? How many hours spent on winning then losing the again. Was there any benefit to my family and friends? How many times did my mind open and close? Is there a particular way the story should go? I do know they all end the same on this plane. In between, was there something I gleaned? Mixed in is happiness and grief while walking the balance beam. Engaging my mind, my hands, legs and my feet. So many culprits along the way. Taking a chance moving from limb to branch. Never calculating the fall, not like leaves fall. My thoughts run rampant at midnight. Less guessing more knowing, showing up in the results. Are gains heavier than losses? Missing turning points, having to deal with what's next. How long will the loss last, after adding a period to time that has gone by. Sometimes the minutes are tricky, making you think you have hours to decide. As the gains go bye, bye, the mind needs the exercise, but not chasing the lost cause. Confident of being certain seeing through the curtain gives the gain an edge. Blind men don't bluff. No short cuts on long runs. My imagination almost stretched to back to yester year. There are no handlebars on fear. Mentors I had, would always ask me, why not? When you drop your guard, inches turn to yards. Liars know the truth, otherwise they couldn't lie. With everything that you've seen, why would you ever ask WHY. Is a gain worth the pain? What is the cost with the loss? Some things are too difficult to measure.

SHHUUH! Be quiet son, don't wake your mother she is sleeping.

hülya n. yılmaz

hülya n. yılmaz

Of Turkish descent, hülya n. yılmaz [sic] is Professor Emerita (Penn State, U.S.A.), Director of Editing Services (Inner Child Press International, U.S.A.), and a trilingual literary translator. Before her poetry and prose publications, she authored an extensive research book in German on cross-cultural literary influences.

Her works of literature include a trilingual collection of poems, memoirs in verse, prose poetry, short stories, a bilingual poetry book, and two books of poetry (one, co-authored). Her poetic offerings appeared in numerous anthologies of global endeavors.

hülya writes creatively to attain and nourish a comprehensive awareness for and development of our humanity.

hülya n. yılmaz, a traveler on the journey called "life" . . .

Writing Web Site
https://hulyanyilmaz.com/

Editing Web Site
https://hulyasfreelancing.com

Child Rape and My Country of Birth*

The news was impossible for me to disregard,
And regarded, I have.
To word my reaction to it as non-fiction, however,
Was a thought far too disturbing to me.

I, a woman having passed her 60s, born into
And raised in modern Turkey before leaving
For the United States of America,
My anon-similarly-tainted-adoptive-country
In pursuit of an advanced academic career
Numerous decades ago.

So,
I have
Resorted
To the infinite
Embrace of ease
And offerings of comfort
That only poetry succeeds to lend.

In my attempt
To at least somewhat forget,
I have called in my all-time favorite poet
To please come to my rescue with his worldly work,
And he, the gracious Nazım Hikmet appeared in my sphere.

While terribly saddened by the latest shock
For his legendarily beloved country of also my birth,
I imagined how this world-renowned exilic Turk would rest
His dire concerns about Turkey's fate
With infinite confidence

In the hands of her women
Who in multiple thousands
Had gathered in a peaceful protest,
And kept marching through the former capital
Going after the proposed Child Sex Law
Not minding the ancient old, hard-to walk-on-streets
That İstanbul, the world's only dual continental-city
Had seen being etched by countless histories in the making.

After Nazım's imagined visit to my library of his books
And following a perusal at ease of his legendary trust
In Turkey's female species he left behind via poetry,
I began to see the thick slices of reassurance
In his persistently prophetic deliberations
Amid his deep-rooted concerns about
The also-back then-objectionable
Status of Turkish women:
Wrongdoings, regardless of their nature
Will persist anywhere in the world. No doubt.
As long as there exist those dear spirits, however
That aim at attaining a balance between the evil and good
There will always be
Hope for all humanity
From this point on
To eternity.

---

*An old poem that first appeared in my *Aflame.Memoirs in Verse*, published on August 2, 2017 by Inner Child Press International.

The Blue-Eyed Giant

Typical Turkish, I'd say . . .

Chastise
Ostracize
Stigmatize
Verbally brutalize
While still amid the living

But
Comprehend
Appreciate
Celebrate
When dead

Nazım

to you, I dedicated many a poem
in my adulthood years, that is

i don't recall
when I first learned your name,
but you were always dressed
inside your posthumous fame

a dear old man once chanted
your lesser-known poems for me,
each of them, off the top of his head

mesmerizingly beautiful his rendition of you was

no matter how young i had ever been,
no poem of yours would come to me in full

your tribute to Turkey's women, however,
i mean, the nameless daughters of Anatolia,
lives in me with such a presence
that neither time nor space can ever erase

KADINLAR
KADINLARIMIZ
SOFRADA YERI . . .

hülya n. yılmaz

Teresa E. Gallion

Teresa E. Gallion

Teresa E. Gallion was born in Shreveport, Louisiana and moved to Illinois at the age of 15. She completed her undergraduate training at the University of Illinois Chicago and received her master's degree in Psychology from Bowling Green State University in Ohio. She retired from New Mexico state government in 2012.

She moved to New Mexico in 1987. While writing sporadically for many years, in 1998 she started reading her work in the local Albuquerque poetry community. She has been a featured reader at local coffee houses, bookstores, art galleries, museums, libraries, Outpost Performance Space, the Route 66 Festival in 2001 and the State of Oklahoma's Poetry Festival in Cheyenne, Oklahoma in 2004. She occasionally hosts an open mic.

Teresa's work is published in numerous Journals and anthologies. She has two CDs: *On the Wings of the Wind* and *Poems from Chasing Light*. She has published three books: *Walking Sacred Ground, Contemplation in the High Desert* and *Chasing Light*.

Chasing Light was a finalist in the 2013 New Mexico/Arizona Book Awards.

The surreal high desert landscape and her personal spiritual journey influence the writing of this Albuquerque poet. When she is not writing, she is committed to hiking the enchanted landscapes of New Mexico. You may preview her work at

http://bit.ly/1aIVPNq or *http://bit.ly/13IMLGh*

Beloved Turkish Poet

Government did not love you
when you were alive.
They imprisoned you
for your communist views
and banned your poetry.

People reading your political poetry
brought you the gift of prison
and exile most of your life.
That did not stop your pen.
Only death achieved that end.

Despite a ban on your poetry until 1965,
A Nobel Peace Prize was received and
recognition as one of the great 20th centuries
international poets.

Your legacy lives into the 21st century
as first modern beloved Turkish poet.

Love Spheres

Nakedness exposes her to the fire of truth.
The heat burns her beyond recognition.
Like a Phoenix, she rises from her ashes
wearing a purple robe.

She writes the rain into her story,
absorbs the moisture to soothe
the heartburn of memories in her bosom.

When she spreads her wings wide,
light floods her space in golden waves.
The radiance lifts her off the ground.
She soars like an eagle in the earth realm.

Nothing will stop her this lifetime.
Pursuit of truth will take her home
riding on the spheres of love.

Mother's Mulch

An autumn seedling takes refuge
in mother's garden.
It provides a protective mulch
that allows autumn drifters
a hibernation space.

Caught in the chill of winter's grip
everything becomes barren and stiff.
White flakes flutter to earth.
The glitter reinforces mother's mulch.

The little seedling, not the least concerned,
turns over and lets out a smug yarn,
curls up for a long peaceful sleep.
A cozy haven of rest is claimed.

Drifters with spring visions
always make claims on mother's mulch.

Ashok K. Bhargava

Ashok K. Bhargava

ASHOK BHARGAVA is a poet, writer, inspirational speaker and a literary consultant. He has attended poetry conferences in Italy, Turkey, India and Philippines. His latest book "Riding the Tide" about his battle with cancer has been translated and published in Arabic, Hindi, Telugu and Bengali languages. He is a contributing writer to several anthologies worldwide including World Poetry Almanac 2014. He has been published in numerous print and online magazines.

Ashok has won many accolades including Poet Ambassador to Japan, Kalidasa International award, World Poetry Lifetime Achievement award, Writers Beyond Borders Peace award and Tapsilog Leadership award for his community involvement. He is founder of Writers International Network Canada Society to discover, nourish, recognize and celebrate writers, poets and artists and to assist them to network with the community at large. He is the author of eight books of poetry and one anthology. He is Artist-in-Residence at Moberly Arts & Cultural Centre and also co-edits the literary section of The Link Newspaper.

Nâzim Hikmet

I admire the way
you hold together under pressure
to face up to your challenges
and rebound.

You're driven
persistent,
and strong.

You are playful
Silly and
fun.

You are
Compassionate
Sympathetic and
understanding.

 You're just plain unstoppable.
And you always have time for others.

Although I know you cannot be found,
you cannot be seen
and if I write you a letter
I'll get no answer
but I will still look for you.

Time To Get Back

It's been long since you called me or
knocked on my door. I don't want to tell

you anything about my despair,
my sleepless nights and gloomy hours

soaked in tears, compelling me to curse
you but I pray for your happiness instead.

It's time to get back to
my gray days, to pour out tenderly

a few drops of light to erase darkness,
to fill up my soul with a ray of sunshine.

I promise I will turn it into a shimmering,
and a magnificent rainbow.

It's Still Worthwhile

Life sucks.
It's so hard to please -
Family. Relatives. Friends
and Bosses.

Nature is in turmoil.
Fires, floods and earthquakes.

But there are many reasons
to be happy and to celebrate -
Sunrise. Sunset.
Music. Books.
Birds. Trees.
And more.
You just have to see
beyond the horizon.

Caroline
'Ceri Naz'
Nazareno
Gabis

Caroline 'Ceri' Nazareno-Gabis

Caroline 'Ceri Naz' Nazareno-Gabis, author of Velvet Passions of Calibrated Quarks, World Poetry Canada International Director to Philippines is a multi-awarded poet, editor, journalist, educator, peace and women's advocate. She believes that learning other's language and culture is a doorway to wisdom.

Among her poetic belts include **Gabrielle Galloni Memorial Panorama International Youth Award** 2022, Panorama Youth Literary Awards 2020, 7th Prize Winner in the 19th, 20th and 21st Italian Award of Literary Festival; Writers International Network-Canada ''Amazing Poet 2015'', The Frang Bardhi Literary Prize 2014 (Albania), Poet Journalist Award 2014 (Tuzla, Istanbul, Turkey) and World Poetry Empowered Poet 2013 (Vancouver, Canada). She's a featured member of Association of Women's Rights and Development (AWID), The Poetry Posse, Galaktika Poetike, Asia Pacific Writers and Translators (APWT), Axlepino and Anacbanua. Her poetry and children's stories have been featured in different anthologies and magazines worldwide.

Links to her works:

http://panitikan.ph/2018/03/30/caroline-nazareno-gabis/

https://apwriters.org/author/ceri_naz/

http://www.aveviajera.org/nacionesunidasdelasletras/id1181.html

State of Freedom
a Tribute to Nazim Hikmet

I can see freedom

Free as the clouds

Hanging up there,

When the sun is up,

His eyes light up cyan straits

Connecting our past to the future,

His glances transcend ivory, silky petals,

Mirror of best days ahead,

Like his favorite Sunday.

I can see freedom,

From the poetry revolts

of Don Quixote,

The tale of an immortal youth.

still

oftentimes I complain
why should I go
under the scorching sun
in the middle of the fields,
causing pain, allergies, uneasiness,
when in the first place,
 I can ride the easiest possible way
to reach my destination;
but the tree as I can see it
standing still, firm and exquisite
reminds me of three e-words:
endure. Entrust. Empower.

Enough

I choose peace

In my daughter's eyes,

Seeing her mother's face painting

Butterfly and fairy,

Playing around with album of stickers,

Sticking Melody and Hello Kitty's dresser,

Just like hugs and kisses,

That stick on her little body and chubby cheeks,

That story is enough to fill the gaps.

Swapna Behera

Swapna Behera is a trilingual poet, translator, environmentalist, editor from India and author of seven books of different genres including one on children's literature on Environment. She is the recipient of International UGADI AWARD 2019, honoured from Gujurat Sahitya Akademi 2022, 2021 International Poesis Award of Honor as Jury, Pentasi B World Fellow Poet, Honoured Poet of India from Seychelles Government and International awards from Algeria, Morocco, Kajhakhstan, modern Arabic Literary Renaissance of Egypt, International Arts Council Argentina etc. Her stories, poems, articles are published in many International and National magazines and ezines. Her poem A NIGHT IN THE REFUGEE CAMP is translated into 67 languages. She has received over 60 National and International Awards. At present she is the Cultural Ambassador for India and South Asia of Inner Child and the life member of Odisha Environmental Society

Email
swapna.behera@gmail.com

Web Site
http://swapnabehera.in/

Nazim Hikmet

the first modern Turkish poet
a journalist, playwright
novelist, scriptwriter and translator
recognized for the lyrical flow of his statement
he was awarded
 the International Peace prize
nazim Hikmet
contributed to the
world peace council
worked for world peace, disarmament
human rights and social justice
worked on Human Landscapes, his magnum opus
living is no laughing matter
we must live as if we will never die
so have to live with great seriousness
"I don't want to listen to songs
I want to sing"
loving you is like living …….

Don't translate me

don't ever try to translate me
I am a river
in ominous blue
you pretend
projects ,seminars
all your intoxicated border lines
how dare you translate me
with your plastic brain and heart
my shore is my own empire
your smiles seldom carry the joy
you dump the garbage , the trash
I try to survive

don't ever try to translate me
I am a tree
standing alone on the highway
I have seen the dances of civilisations
the slices of your own lungs
that need oxygen
I am life unmasked
don't transform me
your parameter is not
the life saving drug for me
I need a life that can stand on the podium bravely

I am a soldier
a blood stream of credibility
all can read but only my country can write upon me
not so easy to sing a song
still difficult to sing the national anthem
don't ever try to translate my soul
every single soul speaks a new language

your version is limited
so stop squeezing the alphabets
they are the mile stones of each song
that none can ever translate

the platter is ready

the platter is ready
to cater unique dish
every illustration is converted
a lover is tossed every second
silky nights are breathless
life is a blast of smouldering embers
the wheel spins
yes the platter is ready
 all seasons
all colours
all infusions
all identities
all territorials
all ideologies
all fantasies
all concepts
march forward towards
the core dialect
that is in sync with
 the fabric of our cosmic nerves
of course the platter is ready
to merge into the galaxy…..

Swapna Behera

Albert 'Infinite' Carrasco

Albert 'Infinite' Carassco

Albert "Infinite The Poet" Carrasco is an urban poet, mentor and public speaker.

Albert believes his experience of growing up in poverty, dealing with drugs and witnessing murder over and over were lessons learnt, in order to gain knowledge to teach. Albert's harsh reality and honesty is a powerfully packed punch delivered through rhyme. Infinite grew up in the east part of the Bronx and still resides there, so he knows many young men will follow the same dark path he followed looking for change. The life of crime should never be an option to being poor but it is, very often.

Infinite poetry @lulu.com

Alcarrasco2 on YouTube

Infinite the poet on reverbnation

Infinite Poetry

www.lulu.com/us/en/shop/al-infinite-carrasco/infinite-poetry/paperback/product-21040240.html

www.innerchildpress.com/albert-carrasco

Nazim Hikmet

I am a Turkish poet, playwright, novelist, screenwriter, director and memoirist born in Greece. Through my writing i share my visions of what life should be and how we should live with love, liberty and peace. I have no filter when it comes to getting my thoughts out on stages or paper, I will be heard. My political views ruffled the feathers of a non communist government, so I was exiled and put in jail as punishment. They've imprisoned my body but my mind roamed free, they put me in a cell but I continued to write because I had knowledge to share and a story to tell. Although I spent most of my adult life in prison I've made my mark in history as being one of the most important and influential figures in the 20th century. I had positive messages to share, I couldn't even be silenced while living in despair. In 1950 when I was released from jail due to the publics and my families outcry's I became a recipient of the international peace prize. I escaped Turkey to Romania, then i moved to the Soviet Union where my works continued to be put in publication.

Horrific Visions

He was right there! Right there on the cold floor. Arms spread out, one leg stretched out the other folded. The gun powder ignited, the slug exploded, blammmmmmmm, I just lost my man.. I want to hold him, pray for him, I want to let him know at this final moment, I'm there for him. Volar sin miedo, go with god, grace el cielo mi hermano.

But but but.. I can't touch him. Why? Because I had skipped a court date running for my freedom, so all I could do was pass in a tinted car and circle the block 100 times looking at this dead friend of mines. " My brother do you see me? My presence is here ,im so very near do you feel me"? That was me trying to connect through ESP. I guess at that time his soul had already flew free because he wasn't responding. I switched over to phd (Power to Hear the Dead) to see if he was reaching out to me, Nothing. At that moment, time must of been rewinding, they say that's what happens before dying. I was too late and too early for a conversation before death and after passing. Paradise was setting in on him, while I was thinking about who ever killed him and when i saw him, how would I introduce him to armageddon. Noooooo, there goes that wagon. Wait wait please please, before for you zip him, let me get one more view of him,I starred as they removed him.... It was bitter sweet. The bitter part is he's dead, the sweet part is hes at rest somewhere out the ghetto..

Me the Devil

I used to wake up to heat, I thought it was the sun but it was the devil at my feet, at every crack of dawn he would be there tempting me. He didn't let me sleep, he was scared that if I reached r e m i would dream of god or the heavens, see angels and talk to them. So he awakened me before seven, he would breathe heavy on me and sixty six other children at six, do ya see the pattern ? He gave us tools of his trade. He said theres money to be made, we listened. In the park were we played we listened to hells serenade as narrated instructions, while covering those actions as kids at play.. A facade. He woke me up to do this for a few decades. All my adolescent thru young adult years... One day at rest I felt the heat I kept my eyes closed struggling to stay asleep... And I did.. I saw myself in a different life... I saw paradise. I saw light... I heard angels.. They told me that they broke curfew to save my life...

Michelle Joan Barulich

Michelle Joan Barulich

Michelle Joan Barulich was born in Honolulu, Hawaii on the island of Oahu. She started writing poetry and songs with her younger brother Paul. They have written many songs in their teen years. She is currently studying Alternative Medicine and would like to become a Homeopathic Doctor. Michelle loves all kinds of animals and birds; she does wild rehabilitation. She has also rescued rock pigeons that make great pets.

https://www.facebook.com/michelle.barulich

Nazim Hikmet

A Turkish poet, playwriter and novelist

You preached for peace and pleaded for safety

Your words were heard

You shined brightly.

As a powerful antiwar message

You stood your ground

You protested and it payed off.

When you were among the recipients of the international peace prize

Your distinguished syllabic poets

You trailblazed in many fields

Your books and poetry legacy still lives on.

Away Unto Me

The light has a secret behind its force
Pictures of life know the meaning
And the flame of the fire know how to throw you off
The moon lit with caution
And every cry you know is heard
And every tear is counted
And every different road we take
Will become as one in the end
Away unto me,
I love
Away unto me
I hate
Away unto me
I wish
The magic of the unicorn
Will steal our hearts
And children will be wise until the end
My hope is like a dream
My dream is something I want to be
The words play an emotion
With every line theirs a feelin
Images reflect in space
A time, I see you
Nine years ago in the past
Away unto me;
Away unto you;
Away unto me and you

What is Love?

I want a friend
That will always be by my side
Love is not a feeling or desire
It's much more than You'll ever know
Love is giving
Real love is not even possible
Without a degree of maturity
Part of it may be biological structure
But it wont get us far enough
We all want a friend
Philadelphia comes into place
Time for brotherly love
Face to face;
Shoulder to shoulder;
We might just make it
Romance and friends are fine
But what I need is a total commitment
But don't marry for convenience
Don't marry for desire or security
Not for money or any other reasons at all
Love never stands still
It begins slowly and grows.

Eliza Segiet

Eliza Segiet graduated with a Master's Degree in Philosophy at Jagiellonian University.

Received *Global Literature Guardian Award* – from Motivational Strips, World Nations Writers Union and Union Hispanomundial De Escritores (UHE) 2018.

Nominated for the Pushcart Prize 2019, 2021.

Laureate *Naji Naaman Literary Prize 2020*,

International Award Paragon of Hope (2020),

World Award 2020 *Cesar Vallejo* for Literary Excellence. Laureate of the Special Jury *Sahitto International Award* 2021, World Award *Premiul Fănuş Neagu* 2021.

Finalist *Golden Aster Book* World Literary Prize 2020, *Mili Dueli* 2022, Voci nel deserto 2022.

At the international Festival of Poetry CAMPIONATO MONDIALE DI POESIA (2021/2022) she won the title of vice-champion of the world.

Award BHARAT RATNA RABINDRANATH TAGORE INTERNATIONAL AWARD (2022).

Award - *World Poets Association* (2023).

Laureate Between words and infinity *"International Literary Award (2023).*

Lost Opportunities
In memory of Nâzım Hikmet

Imprisoned for his views,
deprived of his citizenship for those same reasons.
Was that not enough?
No! He was exiled from Turkey – the country
he never stopped loving,
where his poetry was banned.

When he died, he was granted
what he could no longer appreciate.
Did he have to remain silent
so that the country from which he came
would regain its lost opportunities?

Can anyone read from the content of the poem
his posthumous expectation
that his body, buried in exile,
would one day return to his beloved country?
That's what he wanted and that's what he wrote about.

*Mehmed Nâzım Ran, commonly known as Nâzım Hikmet was a Turkish poet, playwright, novelist, screenwriter, director, memoirist.

Translated by Dorota Stępińska

Respect

For you
it's just a stepping stone from everyday life,
not just verbal games,
fun.
Promises
she believes in naively.
Unnecessarily
you have made an obedient puppet out of her.

You know that
in a woman thirsty for love
one is not allowed
to ignite hope by passion.

Limits of decency
do not require courage
– but respect for the other.

Translated by Artur Komoter

Loss

It's not that
she has stopped thinking about you.
Maybe in your memory
she is wan.

For her
you are still
– not the meaning of existence,
but a warning.

A what? What are you talking about?
I didn't do anything to her.

Apart from the false promises,
you gave her those days
in which you really were.

Although she remembers your touch,
she no longer believes
it was real.

Translated by Artur Komoter

William S. Peters Sr.

William S. Peters, Sr.

Bill's writing career spans a period of well over 50 years. Being first Published in 1972, Bill has since went on to Author in excess of 50+ additional Volumes of Poetry, Short Stories, etc., expressing his thoughts on matters of the Heart, Spirit, Consciousness and Humanity. His primary focus is that of Love, Peace and Understanding!

Bill says . . .

I have always likened Life to that of a Garden. So, for me, Life is simply about the Seeds we Sow and Nourish. All things we "Think and Do", will "Be" Cause and eventually manifest itself to being an "Effect" within our own personal "Existences" and "Experiences" . . . whether it be Fruit, Flowers, Weeds or Barren Landscapes! Bill highly regards the Fruits of his Labor and wishes that everyone would thus go on to plant "Lovely" Seeds on "Good Ground" in their own Gardens of Life!

to connect with Bill, he is all things Inner Child

www.iaminnerchild.com

Personal Web Site

www.iamjustbill.com

The Making of Nâzım Hikmet

I once visited Istanbul
A city that spans 2 continents
I was blessed to taste the culture
That still prevails
To this day
. . . .
There was
Byzantine Hagia Sophia,
The Blue Mosque, the Sultanahmet,
The Hippodrome of Constantine,
The Topkapı Palace,
And so much, much more

In my wanderings of wonder
I thought about the past glory
Of the Ottoman Empire
And all that it spawned
During its time of prevalence
. . . .
The Poets, the Artists
The Musicians, the Soldiers,
The Scribes and the Pious Ones,
The Conquered,
And the Conquerors,
And most of all,
The People

There were voices
That stood at the edge,
The vanguards of sanctity,
The Revolutionaries
Of which

Nâzım Hikmet
Was a precious gem
That yet to this day
Shines and illuminates the way
To a reason
That speaks to an equity
For us all.

You

You are my favorite color,
The reason I believe in rainbows,
Because you, yes you
Are my pot of gold

You must be the reason
That the birds sing to me,
For the glow of you
Is all about me

I care not for horizons
And what may come
For I have you
Right here next to me

Tomorrow as they say
Is but a promise,
And yesterday
Is being forgotten
For I am blinded this day,
And every day
By the light of your presence,
You glow

You are the melody
That gives cause
To my harmony,
And we are the composition
That the masters of music
Seek and sought to express
Yes, you are my reason for rhythm

This breath I breathe
Is laden with the fragrance
Of the makings

Of your heart ... love
....
I am the Spring,
And you are the reason
My flowers bloom
The reason for
The bees and the butterflies
Who exude a wonder
That enlightens evokes,
The giggles and laughter
The souls of the children,
And thus us all

You are so much more
Than these simple words
And I am too simple
Of Mind and of heart
To capture the rapture
Of our life-embrace

I look into your eyes
And I become lost
In the depths of expectation
Of what we may yet become ...
Unsettling delicious

You are my inspiration,
The summation
Of my elation

You, you, you
Silence me, my angst,
For in your heart
Is where I wish to
Eternally dwell .
.... You

A Sunday Morning Reflection

It was 1994
Or something like that,
A time so long ago

I was younger then,
Well of course I was,
I even laughed
So much more ....
Of course I did
For there were far less aches and pains

I would like to think
I have become a bit wiser,
But that appears to be
In suspect,
For there are still small issues
That trouble me
That i can not fully resolve,
So I keep burying them
Deeper

I still lament the loss of loved ones,
Some moreso than others,
But though the pain is
Not quite as acute
As it used to be,
That shit still ain't cute;
So once again
I just dig the hole
A bit deeper
To bury my unresolved anguish

Funny, amusing even,
How counselors and priests
And friends and charlatans

All espouse
That they know the way
To salvation ....
Well I listened often,
Why hell, I even followed a few
Until we arrived at that cliff
Where they encouraged
Everyone except themselves
To jump off
.....
Hah, I see myself as somewhat
Smarter than that!
.....
Sometimes I consider
What did lie
At the bottom
Is it any different
From the bottomless pits
Of my life
That I have frequented
From time to time
During this journey
We deem 'life'?

I often wonder
To what end
Do these personal examinations
Deliver my wayward soul unto?
......
I still find joy
In the laughter of children
And adults as well;
I still enjoy the seasonal grandeur
Of the Spring, Summer, Autumn and Winter,
But as I ingest these moments
Which create memories,

I ask,
Can I take them with me
To the next lifetime?

There is so much more
That i have to think about,
Surmise,
But far too often,
I close my eyes
To the possibilities
Of the evolution
That remains before me
For I find myself sitting here
Contemplating, judging
Without any finite commitment

Am I wiser?
Than I was on 1994?
Hah ....
Why bother I say.

That cliff still remains
For those who would consider
It as an alternative ...
Me, i am satisfied
To sit here
And immerse myself in
A Sunday Morning Reflection

March 2024 Featured Poets

Francesco Favetta

Jagjit Singh Zandu

Carmela Núñez Yukimura Peruana

Michael Lee Johnson

Francesco Favetta

Francesco Favetta

The poet Francesco Favetta was born in Sicily in Sciacca, he has always loved poetry, writing verses, but above all culture, food for the soul: culture is Freedom, it is Free Spirit, it is Soul in Movement, not it should never be harnessed! In 2018 he was awarded by the Accademia di Sicilia, Academician of Sicily. He has been published in various anthologies and in various magazines, among which, we mention a few: international magazine The Poet; Revista Azahar who edited the first Sylloge of Poems in Spanish: Encantamiento y Palabras como Plumas; Anthology The Silk Road Anthology: Nano Poems for Africa; "Poetic Galaxy Atunis"; WorldSmith International Editorial; OPA The Poetry Journal; Inumbrable magazine; Magazine Polis; rank of minister in the Order of the Titan and publication of a lyric in Octobermania; international literary magazine Kavya Kishor in Bangladesh; international journal of language, literature and culture "Petrushka Nastamba" Serbia; international magazine, Namaste India and Certificate of Appreciation; Different Truths social journalism platform; Cisne Magazine Digital; Humanity St. Petersburg magazine; fourth Panorama International Literature Festival Spain, delegate for Italy. He founded a theater company in Sciacca: "Theatrum Socialis Sciacca", and a Lions Club, the "Sciacca Terme". Finally, the poet Francesco Favetta is convinced that poetry will be the weapon with which humanity will make their lives free, and furthermore beauty will always be a truth that will never be buried: from the times and events of daily human life!
Francesco Favetta Sciacca (Sicily)

Always sing soul !

And despite everything
life goes on
the world does not stop living
and the answers are close
in the silence of these days
in this song without the voices
in the passages of history
anchors in the wounds of time.
Awake life
enamored creature
fond memory of the poem
and precious dreams
docile majesty in the heart
enchantment in the eyes
you breathe inside the roses in the night
chains broken by courage.
Always sing soul
never stop
give reasons
timeless songs
shout the truths to the world
always be a beacon in the fog
safe harbor and island in the desert
of this heavy sea.

Who we are ?

Who we are
because we don't see
with the eyes
of the soul
reality
and indifference.
Still
behind the wall
of extinguished reason
we pray
with joined hands
that God who
he has to help
our days.
Where
our love
where free thought
he is exiled
in which cave
the consciences
they were locked up.
Along the coasts
of life
vaguely every man
staggering walks
around a temple
beyond which
the flesh transfigures
in a thousand words
and endless poems.

There will be no one left

Who will stay
after the storm
only
shipwrecked and missing
in the raging sea
of human complacency
in everyday violence
in the fences of the world.
And then again
the wars
the divisions
invisible borders
and the truths torn apart
everyday.
Will remain
the blood spilled
from the innocents
and dirty hands
and smelling of death
of criminals
evil humans
sitting in the benches.

Jagjit Singh Zandu

Jagjit Singh Zandu

Jagjit Siingh Zandu (Jit) is a bilingual poet from Punjab(India). He served as Lecturer in Commerce at Government of Punjab for 32 years. He has published an anthology of English poems titled as : "Journey of Love to Salvation ". More than 60 English poems of his, have been published in "ourpoetrycorner@wordpress.com" and also found space in about three dozen international anthologies. His poems are about worldly & divine love but philosophical in nature. His English & Punjabi poems were included in the International Peace Poetathon in Greece, as organized by Dr Chryssa Vellisaiou through video presentation in September 2013, 2014 & 2015. His 2nd anthology of poems "A UNIVERSE WITHIN" is being published and is expected to come in hands of readers very soon.

Money Game & The Poor

Money game is a crucial game
For all pleasures & comforts of life
None is fool if one may think
Neither for fame nor for agony

May be the poor or the rich
All are playing at the same pitch
May bread & butter be alluring
But the dogs also stay barking

Everything here is an illusion
Blending the accessories so well
One can't even think of any fusion
Police & the thieves feel in heaven

Poor dancing-girls or young lads
Sipping their tears on beats of music
Spoiled rich lads play with guns
Taking the dancers on stage as chicks

Not any festival nor any crowds
It is the tale of sorrows to be sort
Ancient Kings looted public wealth
For places to live lavish & lustrous life

Time has changed so the modes of loot
The commons stay starving in slums
Democracy smiles with its vote power
No one bothers to care the ethics towers
©Jagjit Singh Jandu(Jit)

A Mother's Wish

Being your mother earth
I expect that my kids
Do care for my being
And offer me all health care
That I need to enjoy
The cooling affection of
The velvet of vegetation & forests
Do your duty to save me
from cruel hands
that play
Unfairly for their vested interest
My lungs get suffocated
When you burn stable in
fields
You commit sins making excuses
You kill my friends & churn my chest
Be a real friend for the next harvest
Don't chop off my sloppy breasts
To feed the giant of your greed
To grow the concrete forests
Over the foothill's palms
Never forget, these are my feet
To hug towering Deodars & Pine tree
Which stand tall and strong
To cater all around development
And search the space far beyond

Night Verse

It may be
After midnight
Sound sleep seldom visits me.

I noticed
A verse was strolling
And just stopped by my side

It tried
To converse with it
Told, "I am to give you company."

I requested
Please relax here a little
And we shall talk at sunrise!

It listened
But kept mum as I was sleepy
I searched at dawn but in vain!

I felt sad
As it happens almost every night
But it keeps me busy without work!

My dreams
May help me to concede
If my verses befriend their beauty!

Carmela Núñez Yukimura

Peruana

Carmela Núñez Yukimura Peruana

BIOGRAFÍA DEL AUTOR
Carmela Núñez Yukimura peruana,
Resido : Utah-EEUU.
Autodidacta : poesía,pintura
Profesora jubilada : Lengua, Literatura, Filosofía, Expresión Artística (Peru)
Logros :
2021 -Embajadora Itinerante : CONLEAM
-"Gestor Internacional de Paz" :
Utopía Poética Universal ,los Poetas más grandes del Mundo .
-"Premio Pacifista Global : :Poetas Intergalácticos .
2022"Globo de Cristal" ,"Grito Cultural" "Embajador Cultural " : Plumas y Letras de Curumani .
-Directora Ejecutiva CONLEAM -
-Embajadora Emérito Colegiado CONLEAM
-Embajadora Itinerante de la Paz CONLEAM
-"Medalla de Cultura "Asociación Latinoamericana de Poetas,Artistas (Peru)
-"Medalla de Cultura " Municipalidad Provincial de Arequipa Peru
2023-"Embajador Honoraria Cultural Universal " REALIZAR LA PAZ-
-"Medalla Internacional" Miguel de Cervantes Saavedra .

La Paz Esperanza Del Mañana

Llegan tormentos en los valles del alma
Son dolores que destruyen sueños
De niños,jóvenes,adultos,viejos que lloran:
Por guerras,muertes …sólo desean Paz.

Se sienten preguntas en corazones nuestros
Sangran recuerdos de otros tiempos
Retumban tristezas en tumbas de fuegos
Sólo el alma mira un cielo azul de esperanzas nuevas.

Necesitamos pedir luz brillante a Dios
Que nos aliente a ser ingenieros de Paz
Que nos enseñe a vivir con humildad
A perdonar con amor , fe, solidaridad .

Que donde viva el odio se siembre amor
Donde subsista el desánimo,exista esperanza
Donde habiten tristezas demos alegría y paz al alma
Donde exista arte haya luz en los pueblos del alba
Para que nuestro mundo cada día sea mejor
Sin importar religión , color , raza
Que lo más valioso es el respeto a la hermandad
Sin secretos , Sin poderes , sin glorias
Entendiendo que La Paz es…la esperanza del mañana
Sintiendo al fin una nueva libertad .
Derechos reservados.

El Libro De Mis Sueños

Las hojas de mis versos
Deambulan en papeles arrojados al viento
En llamaradas donde se esfuman recuerdos
Que transcurren débiles en el trajinar del tiempo.
Desde niña escribía versos
Empapelados se reían en el basurero,
No entendía la nostalgia, el llanto
Del amor por escribir en un libro mis versos.
Pasan años en tableros enjaulados
Con apetitos ajenos en soledades al vuelo
Con ambiciones estrelladas en el firmamento
Sin poder escribir en un libro…un verso.
Necesito despertar mi mente
Expresar mis sentimientos ,mis emociones
Abriendo mi alma a esperanzas nuevas
Creando un estilo de vivencias bellas
Así el mundo entenderá mis pensamientos
Guardados en la corteza de mis sentimientos
Hoy…rompiendo el pavimento de ideas dormidas
Dándole al alma un respiro
Desgarraré la cáscara del nido escondido
Escribiré en un buen libro …mis versos perdidos.
Derechos reservados.

Carmela Núñez Yukimura Peruana

Unidos Por Amor

Cierro mis ojos con el aroma de tus besos
Besos de fuego que me atrapan en silencio
Como agujetas de cristal clavando en mi pecho
Deshojando así caricias en mis versos.
La sensualidad de tu alma
Invaden mis suspiros al viento
Caigo rendida en fantasías dormidas
Advirtiendo coloquios apasionados
Hasta el infinito de mis pensamientos .
Detengo el tiempo y vuelo a tus brazos
Sintiendo suspiros del alma
Una noche estrellada bajo la luna plateada
Donde triunfa el hechizo de tu sonrisa
Confesando escondidos secretos
Agradeciendo a Dios por la vida
Brindándonos unión que nos encamina.
En el valle de tus ojos negros
Se dibuja la sensualidad de tu voz
Navegando en delirios de mar abierto
Enseñoreando al mundo cuánto yo te quiero.
Tú…amante de la entrega en silencio
Seduces el cause de mis besos
Te entregas a mi mar de encantos
En suaves tertulias de amor sincero
Cargados de pasiones sin frenos
Por el amor que desfogas muy dentro.
Si…no existen horizontes sin flores
Cuando el amor es verdadero
Sin agonías de falsos recuerdos
Sólo existen suspiros de paz en el alma
En trémulas ternuras por esta unión
Hacia una vida eterna .
Derechos reservados.

Michael

Lee

Johnson

Michael Lee Johnson

Michael Lee Johnson lived ten years in Canada during the Vietnam era. Today he is a poet in the greater Chicagoland area, IL. He has 293 YouTube poetry videos. Michael Lee Johnson is an internationally published poet in 44 countries, a song lyricist, has several published poetry books, has been nominated for 6 Pushcart Prize awards, and 6 Best of the Net nominations. He is editor-in-chief of 3 poetry anthologies, all available on Amazon, and has several poetry books and chapbooks. He has over 472 published poems. Michael is the administrator of 6 Facebook Poetry groups. Member Illinois State Poetry Society: http://www.illinoispoets.org/. Do not forget to consider me for Best of the Net or Pushcart nomination!

Summer is Dying

Outside, summer is dying into fall,

and blue daddy petunias sprout ears—

hear the beginning of night chills.

In their yellow window box,

they cuddle up and fear death together.

The balcony sliding door

is poorly insulated, and a cold draft

creeps into all the spare rooms.

Bowl of Black Petunias

If you must leave me, please
leave me for something special,
like a beautiful bowl of black petunias—
for when the memories leak
and cracks appear
and old memories fade,
flowers rebuff bloom,
sidewalks fester weeds
and we both lie down
separately from each other
for the very last time.

Memories Past
Hillbilly Daddy

I settle into my thoughts
zigzagging between tears
my fathers' grave—
Tippecanoe River
Indiana 1982.
Over now,
a hillbilly country
like the flow
catfish memories
raccoons in trees
coon dogs tracking
on the river bank,
the hunt.
Snapping turtles
in the boat
offline—
river flakes
to ice—
now covered
thick snow.

Remembering

our fallen soldiers of verse

Janet Perkins Caldwell
February 14, 1959 ~ September 20, 2016

Alan W. Jankowski
16 March 1961 ~ 10 March 2017

The Butterfly Effect

"IS" in effect

Inner Child Press

News

Published Books
by
Poetry Posse Members

We are so excited to share and announce a few of the current books, as well as the new and upcoming books of some of our Poetry Posse authors.

On the following pages we present to you ...

Alicja Maria Kuberska
Jackie Davis Allen
Gail Weston Shazor
hülya n. yılmaz
Nizar Sartawi
Elizabeth E. Castillo
Faleeha Hassan
Fahredin Shehu
Kimberly Burnham
Caroline 'Ceri' Nazareno
Eliza Segiet
Teresa E. Gallion
William S. Peters, Sr.

Now Available

www.innerchildpress.com

The Year of the Poet XI ~ March 2024

Once upon a Time in Turkey

hülya n. yılmaz

Now Available
www.innerchildpress.com

Inner Child Press News

Now Available
www.innerchildpress.com

The Year of the Poet XI ~ March 2024

Now Available
www.innerchildpress.com

Inner Child Press News

Now Available
www.innerchildpress.com

The Year of the Poet XI ~ March 2024

Now Available
www.innerchildpress.com

Inner Child Press News

Now Available
www.innerchildpress.com

The Year of the Poet XI ~ March 2024

Now Available
www.innerchildpress.com

Now Available at
www.amazon.com/gp/product/B08MYL5B7S/ref=
dbs_a_def_rwt_hsch_vapi_tkin_p1_i2

The Year of the Poet XI ~ March 2024

Now Available at
www.innerchildpress.com

Inner Child Press News

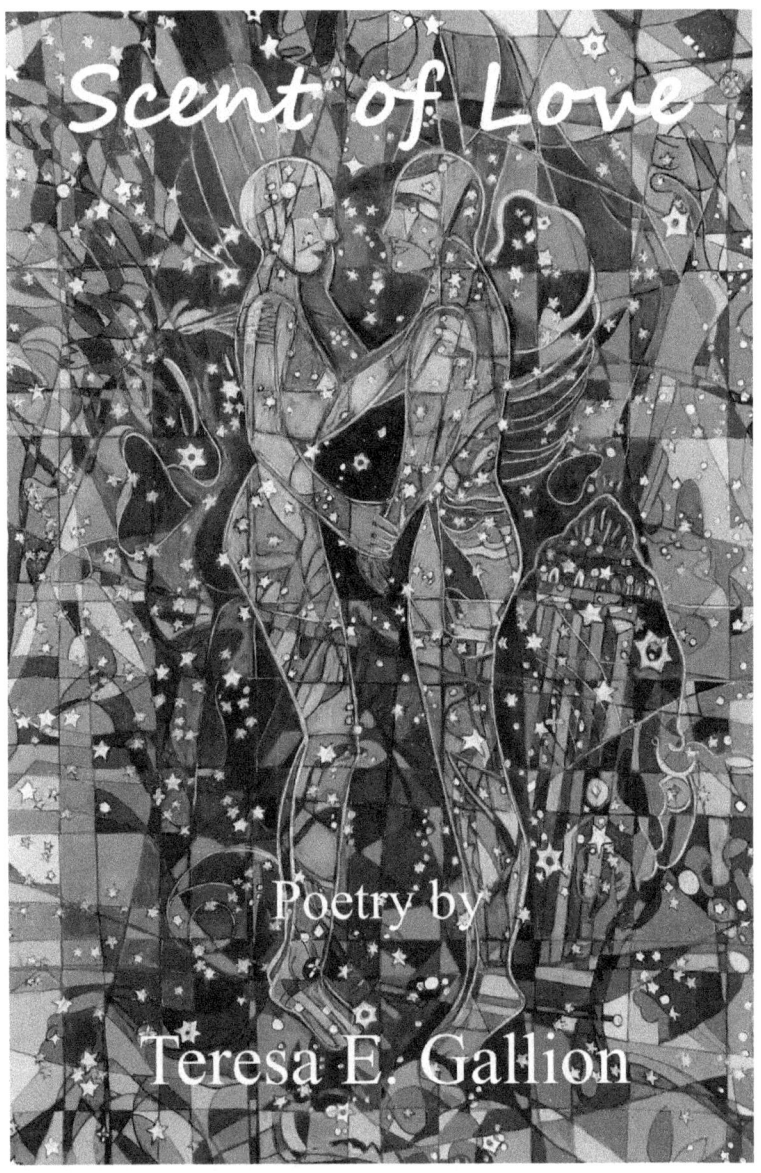

Now Available
www.innerchildpress.com

The Year of the Poet XI ~ March 2024

Now Available
www.innerchildpress.com

Inner Child Press News

Now Available
www.innerchildpress.com

The Year of the Poet XI ~ March 2024

Now Available
www.innerchildpress.com

Now Available
www.innerchildpress.com

The Year of the Poet XI ~ March 2024

The Book of krisar
volume v

william s. peters, sr.

Now Available
www.innerchildpress.com

Inner Child Press News

The Book of krisar
Volume I

william s. peters, sr.

The Book of krisar
Volume II

william s. peters, sr.

Now Available
www.innerchildpress.com

The Book of krisar
Volume III

william s. peters, sr.

The Book of krisar
Volume IV

william s. peters, sr.

Now Available
www.innerchildpress.com

The Year of the Poet XI ~ March 2024

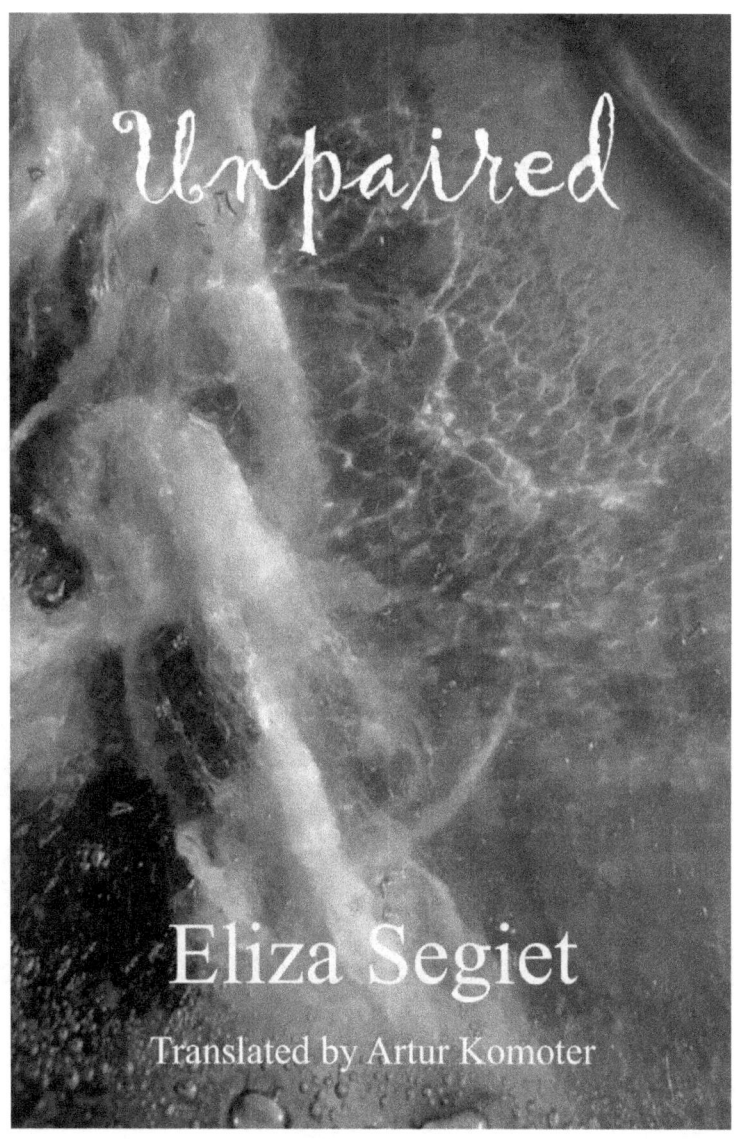

Unpaired

Eliza Segiet

Translated by Artur Komoter

Private Issue
www.innerchildpress.com

Inner Child Press News

Now Available
www.innerchildpress.com

The Year of the Poet XI ~ March 2024

Now Available at
www.innerchildpress.com

Inner Child Press News

Now Available at
www.innerchildpress.com

The Year of the Poet XI ~ March 2024

Now Available at
www.innerchildpress.com

Now Available at
www.innerchildpress.com

The Year of the Poet XI ~ March 2024

HERENOW

FAHREDIN SHEHU

Now Available at
www.innerchildpress.com

Inner Child Press News

Now Available at
www.innerchildpress.com

The Year of the Poet XI ~ March 2024

Dark Side of the Moon

Jackie Davis Allen

Now Available at
www.innerchildpress.com

Inner Child Press News

Now Available at
www.innerchildpress.com

The Year of the Poet XI ~ March 2024

Now Available at
www.innerchildpress.com

Inner Child Press News

Now Available at
www.innerchildpress.com

The Year of the Poet XI ~ March 2024

Breakfast
for
Butterflies

Faleeha Hassan

Now Available at
www.innerchildpress.com

Inner Child Press News

Now Available at
www.innerchildpress.com

The Year of the Poet XI ~ March 2024

Now Available at
www.innerchildpress.com

Inner Child Press News

Now Available at
www.innerchildpress.com

The Year of the Poet XI ~ March 2024

Other

Anthological

works from

Inner Child Press International

www.innerchildpress.com

Inner Child Press Anthologies

Now Available
www.worldhealingworldpeacepoetry.com

Inner Child Press Anthologies

Now Available
www.worldhealingworldpeacepoetry.com

Inner Child Press Anthologies

Now Available
www.innerchildpress.com

Inner Child Press Anthologies

Inner Child Press International
&
The Year of the Poet
present

Poetry
the best of 2020

Poets of the World

Now Available
www.innerchildpress.com

Inner Child Press Anthologies

Now Available
www.innerchildpress.com

Inner Child Press Anthologies

Inner Child Press Anthologies

Now Available
www.innerchildpress.com

Inner Child Press Anthologies

Now Available at
www.innerchildpress.com

Inner Child Press Anthologies

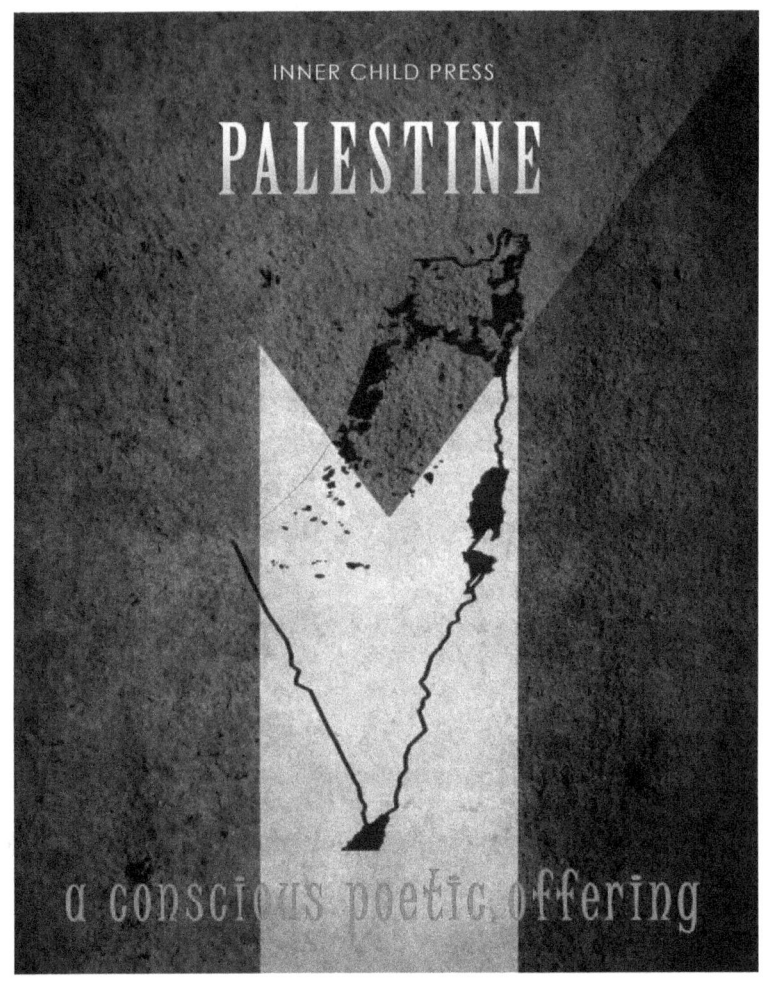

Now Available at
www.innerchildpress.com

Inner Child Press Anthologies

Now Available at
www.innerchildpress.com

Inner Child Press Anthologies

Now Available
www.worldhealingworldpeacepoetry.com

Inner Child Press Anthologies

Now Available
www.worldhealingworldpeacepoetry.com

Inner Child Press Anthologies

Now Available
www.worldhealingworldpeacepoetry.com

Inner Child Press Anthologies

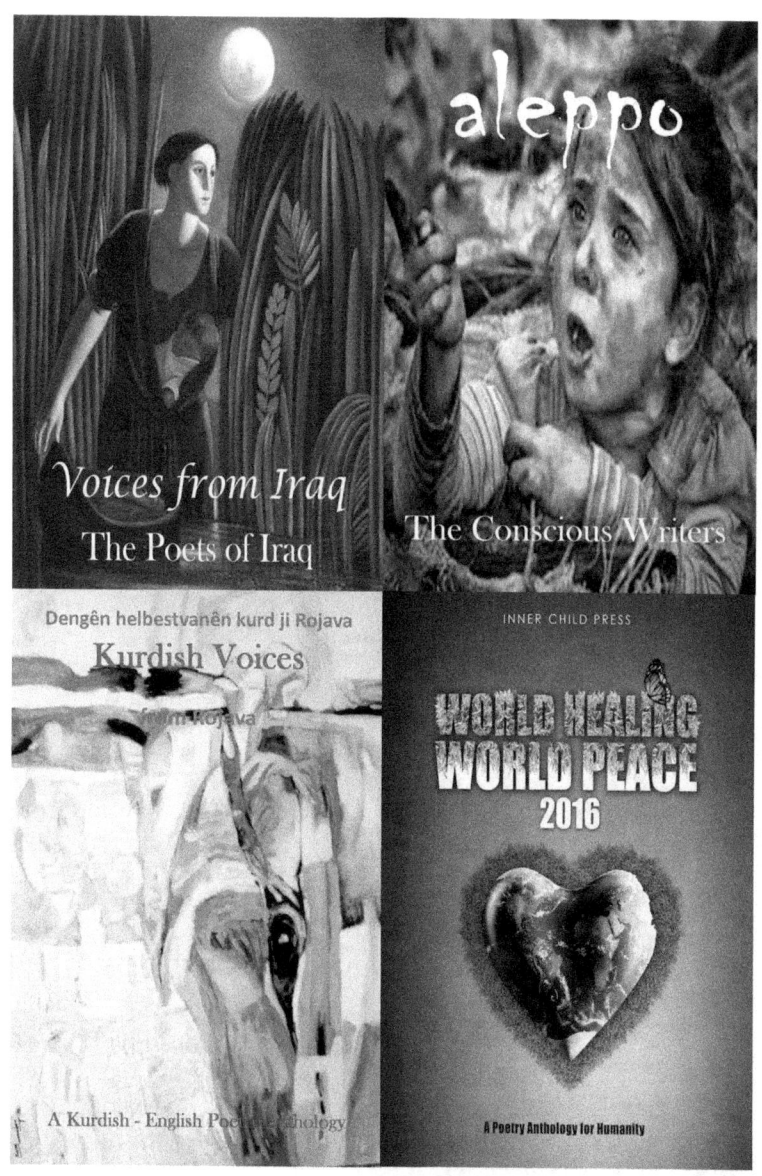

Now Available
www.innerchildpress.com/anthologies

Inner Child Press Anthologies

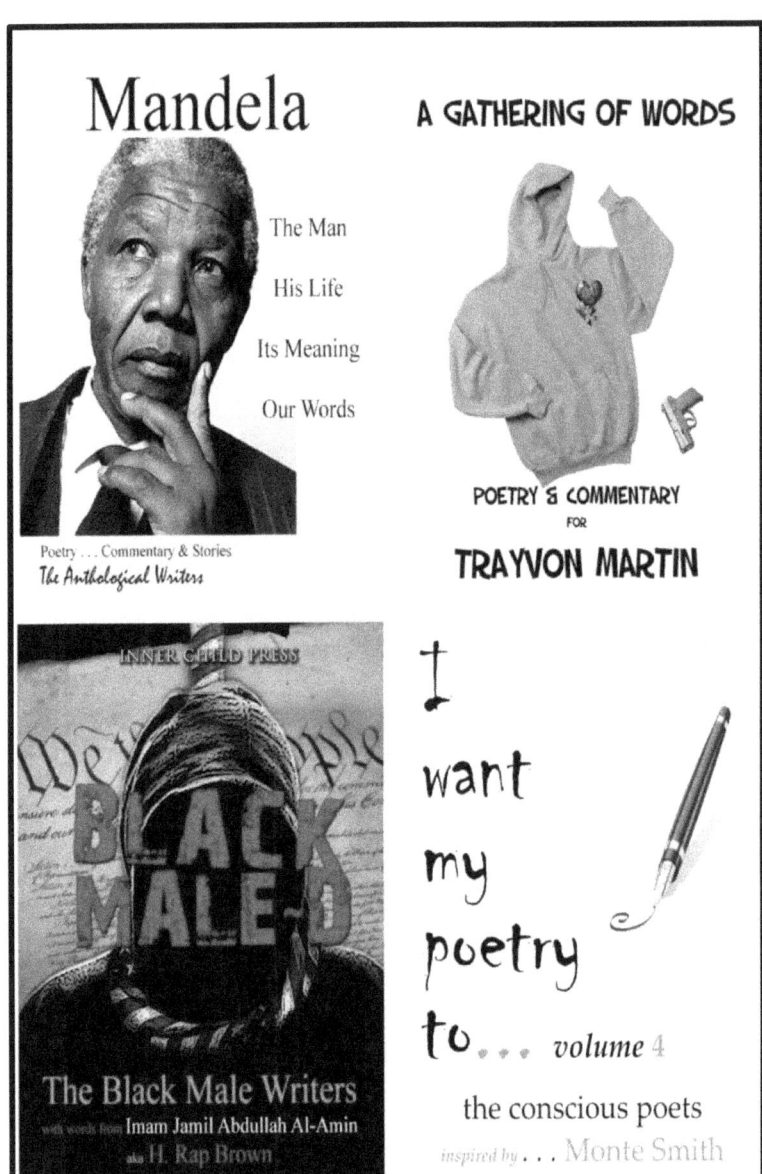

Now Available
www.innerchildpress.com/anthologies

Inner Child Press Anthologies

Now Available
www.innerchildpress.com/anthologies

Inner Child Press Anthologies

Now Available
www.innerchildpress.com/anthologies

Inner Child Press Anthologies

Now Available
www.innerchildpress.com/anthologies

Inner Child Press Anthologies

Now Available
www.innerchildpress.com/the-year-of-the-poet

Inner Child Press Anthologies

Now Available
www.innerchildpress.com/the-year-of-the-poet

Inner Child Press Anthologies

Now Available
www.innerchildpress.com/the-year-of-the-poet

Inner Child Press Anthologies

Now Available

www.innerchildpress.com/the-year-of-the-poet

Inner Child Press Anthologies

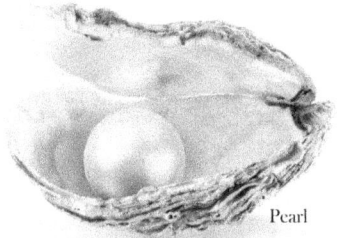

Now Available

www.innerchildpress.com/the-year-of-the-poet

Inner Child Press Anthologies

Now Available
www.innerchildpress.com/the-year-of-the-poet

Now Available
www.innerchildpress.com/the-year-of-the-poet

Inner Child Press Anthologies

Now Available
www.innerchildpress.com/the-year-of-the-poet

Inner Child Press Anthologies

Now Available
www.innerchildpress.com/the-year-of-the-poet

Inner Child Press Anthologies

Now Available
www.innerchildpress.com/the-year-of-the-poet

Inner Child Press Anthologies

Now Available
www.innerchildpress.com/the-year-of-the-poet

Inner Child Press Anthologies

The Year of the Poet IV
September 2017

Featured Poets
Martina Reisz Newberry
Ameer Nassir
Christine Fulco Neal
Robert Neal

The Elm Tree

The Poetry Posse 2017

Gail Weston Shazor * Caroline Nazareno * Bismay Mohanty
Teresa E. Gallion * Anna Jakubczak Vel Ratty Adalan
Joe DaVerbal Minddancer * Shareef Abdur – Rasheed
Albert Carrasco * Kimberly Burnham * Elizabeth Castillo
Hülya N. Yılmaz * Faleeha Hassan * Jackie Davis Allen
Jen Walls * Nizar Sartawi * William S. Peters, Sr.

The Year of the Poet IV
October 2017

Featured Poets
Ahmed Abu Saleem
Nedal Al-Qaeim
Sadeddin Shahin

The Black Walnut Tree

The Poetry Posse 2017

Gail Weston Shazor * Caroline Nazareno * Bismay Mohanty
Teresa E. Gallion * Anna Jakubczak Vel Ratty Adalan
Joe DaVerbal Minddancer * Shareef Abdur – Rasheed
Albert Carrasco * Kimberly Burnham * Elizabeth Castillo
Hülya N. Yılmaz * Faleeha Hassan * Jackie Davis Allen
Jen Walls * Nizar Sartawi * * William S. Peters, Sr.

The Year of the Poet IV
November 2017

Featured Poets
Kay Peters
Alfreda D. Ghee
Gabriella Garofalo
Rosemary Cappello

The Tree of Life

The Poetry Posse 2017

Gail Weston Shazor * Caroline Nazareno * Bismay Mohanty
Teresa E. Gallion * Anna Jakubczak Vel Ratty Adalan
Joe DaVerbal Minddancer * Shareef Abdur – Rasheed
Albert Carrasco * Kimberly Burnham * Elizabeth Castillo
Hülya N. Yılmaz * Faleeha Hassan * Jackie Davis Allen
Jen Walls * Nizar Sartawi * William S. Peters, Sr.

The Year of the Poet IV
December 2017

Featured Poets
Justice Clarke
Mariel M. Pabroa
Kiley Brown

The Fig Tree

The Poetry Posse 2017

Gail Weston Shazor * Caroline Nazareno * Bismay Mohanty
Teresa E. Gallion * Anna Jakubczak Vel Ratty Adalan
Joe DaVerbal Minddancer * Shareef Abdur – Rasheed
Albert Carrasco * Kimberly Burnham * Elizabeth Castillo
Hülya N. Yılmaz * Faleeha Hassan * Jackie Davis Allen
Jen Walls * Nizar Sartawi * William S. Peters, Sr.

Now Available
www.innerchildpress.com/the-year-of-the-poet

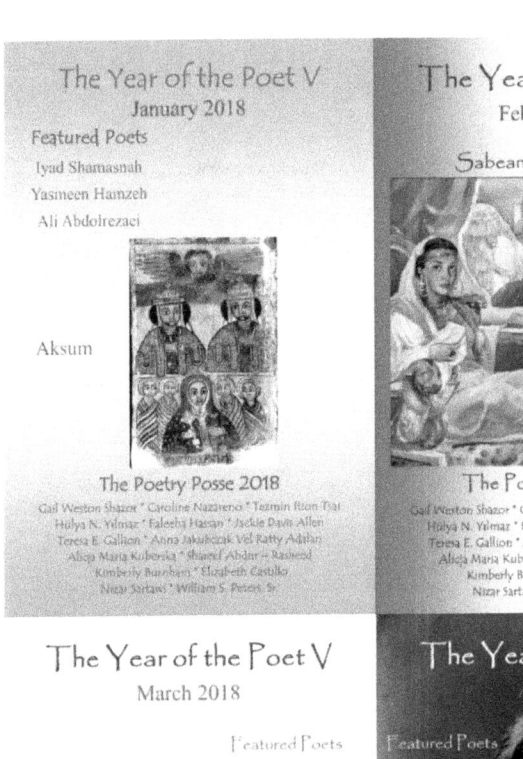
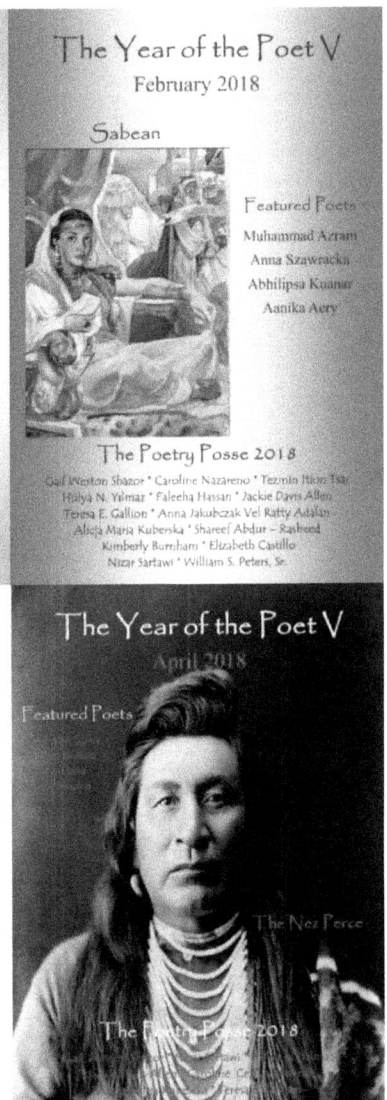

Now Available
www.innerchildpress.com/the-year-of-the-poet

Inner Child Press Anthologies

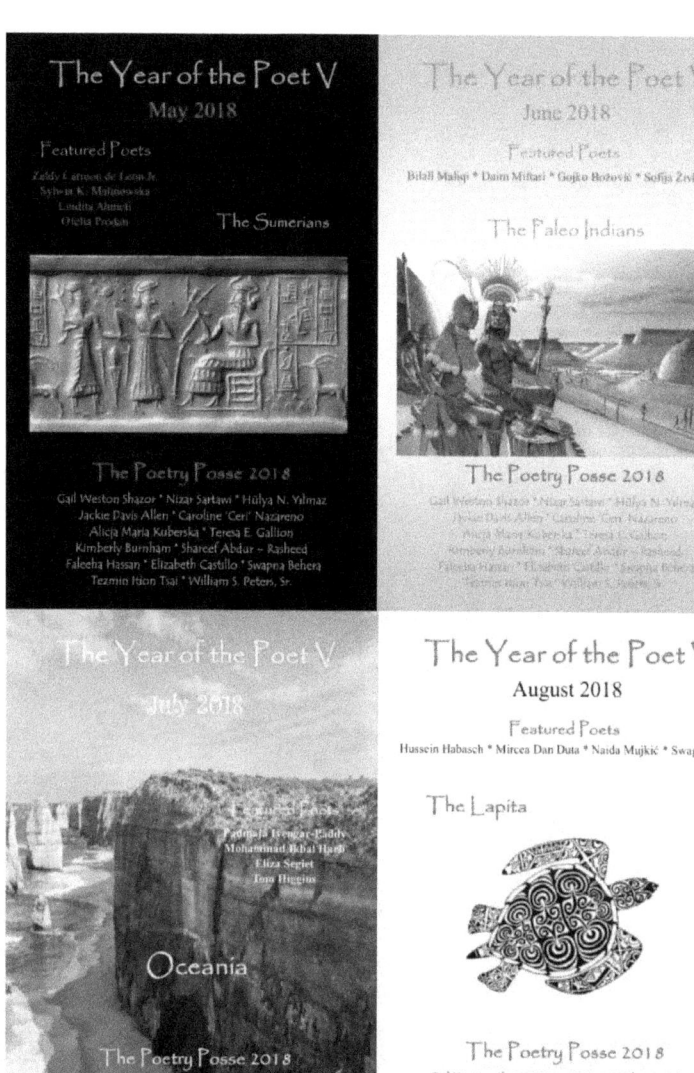

Now Available
www.innerchildpress.com/the-year-of-the-poet

Inner Child Press Anthologies

Now Available
www.innerchildpress.com/the-year-of-the-poet

Inner Child Press Anthologies

The Year of the Poet VI
January 2019

Indigenous North Americans

Featured Poets

Honda Elfchtali
Anthony Briscoe
Iram Fatima 'Ashi'
Dr. K. K. Mathew

Dream Catcher

The Poetry Posse 2019

Gail Weston Shazor * Albert Carrasco * Hülya N. Yilmaz
Jackie Davis Allen * Caroline Nazareno * Eliza Segiet
Alicja Maria Kuberska * Teresa E. Gallion
Kimberly Burnham * Shareef Abdur – Rasheed
Ashok K. Bhargava * Elizabeth Castillo * Swapna Behera
Tezmin Ition Tsai * William S. Peters, Sr.

The Year of the Poet VI
February 2019

Featured Poets
Marek Lukaszewicz * Bharati Nayak
Aida G. Roque * Jean-Jacques Fournier

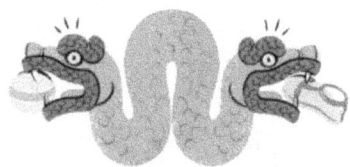

Meso-America

The Poetry Posse 2019

Gail Weston Shazor * Albert Carrasco * Hülya N. Yilmaz
Jackie Davis Allen * Caroline Nazareno * Eliza Segiet
Alicja Maria Kuberska * Teresa E. Gallion * Joe Paire
Kimberly Burnham * Shareef Abdur – Rasheed
Ashok K. Bhargava * Elizabeth Castillo * Swapna Behera
Tezmin Ition Tsai * William S. Peters, Sr.

The Year of the Poet VI
March 2019

Featured Poets
Eniola Mahroof * Sylwia K. Malinowska
Shurouk Hammoud * Anwer Ghani

The Caribbean

The Poetry Posse 2019

Gail Weston Shazor * Albert Carrasco * Hülya N. Yilmaz
Jackie Davis Allen * Caroline Nazareno * Eliza Segiet
Alicja Maria Kuberska * Teresa E. Gallion * Joe Paire
Kimberly Burnham * Shareef Abdur – Rasheed
Ashok K. Bhargava * Elizabeth Castillo * Swapna Behera
Tezmin Ition Tsai * William S. Peters, Sr.

The Year of the Poet VI
April 2019

Featured Poets
DL Davis * Michelle Joan Barulich
Lulëzim Haziri * Faleeha Hassan

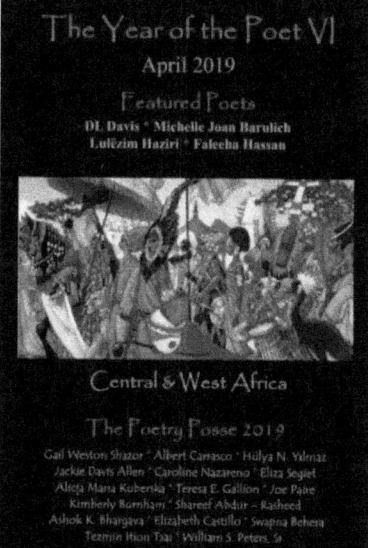

Central & West Africa

The Poetry Posse 2019

Gail Weston Shazor * Albert Carrasco * Hülya N. Yilmaz
Jackie Davis Allen * Caroline Nazareno * Eliza Segiet
Alicja Maria Kuberska * Teresa E. Gallion * Joe Paire
Kimberly Burnham * Shareef Abdur – Rasheed
Ashok K. Bhargava * Elizabeth Castillo * Swapna Behera
Tezmin Ition Tsai * William S. Peters, Sr.

Now Available
www.innerchildpress.com/the-year-of-the-poet

Inner Child Press Anthologies

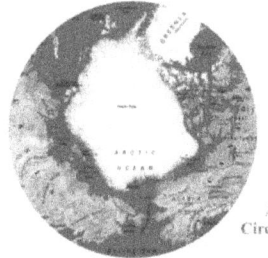

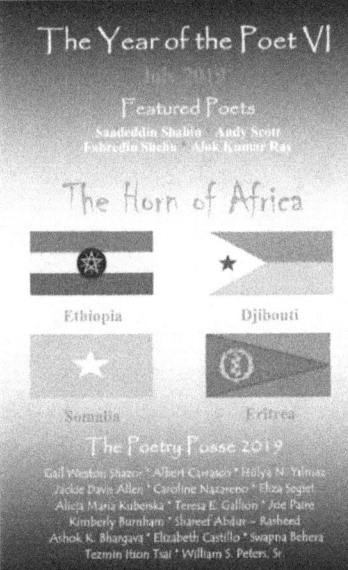

Now Available
www.innerchildpress.com/the-year-of-the-poet

Inner Child Press Anthologies

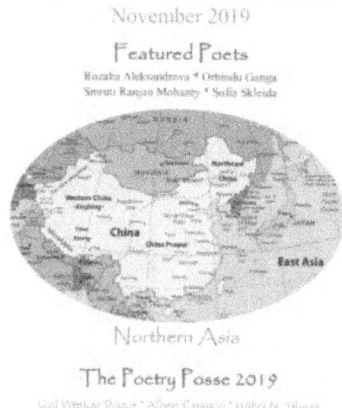

Now Available
www.innerchildpress.com/the-year-of-the-poet

Inner Child Press Anthologies

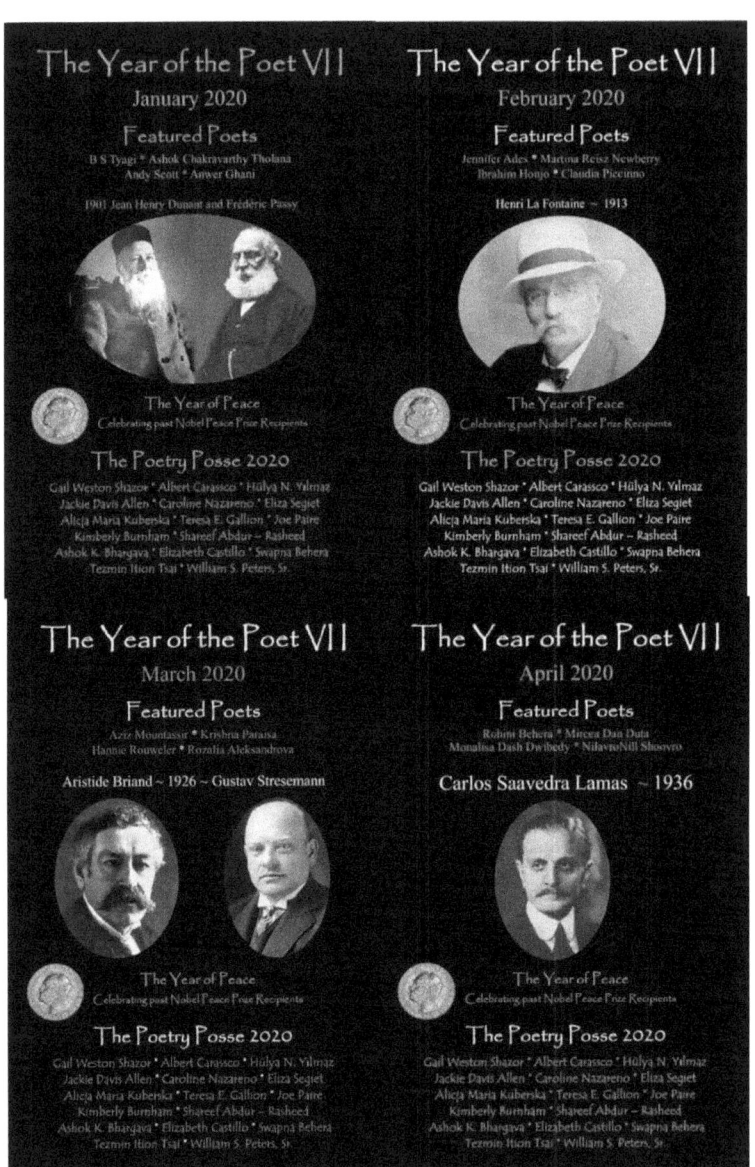

Now Available
www.innerchildpress.com/the-year-of-the-poet

Inner Child Press Anthologies

Now Available
www.innerchildpress.com/the-year-of-the-poet

Inner Child Press Anthologies

Now Available
www.innerchildpress.com/the-year-of-the-poet

Inner Child Press Anthologies

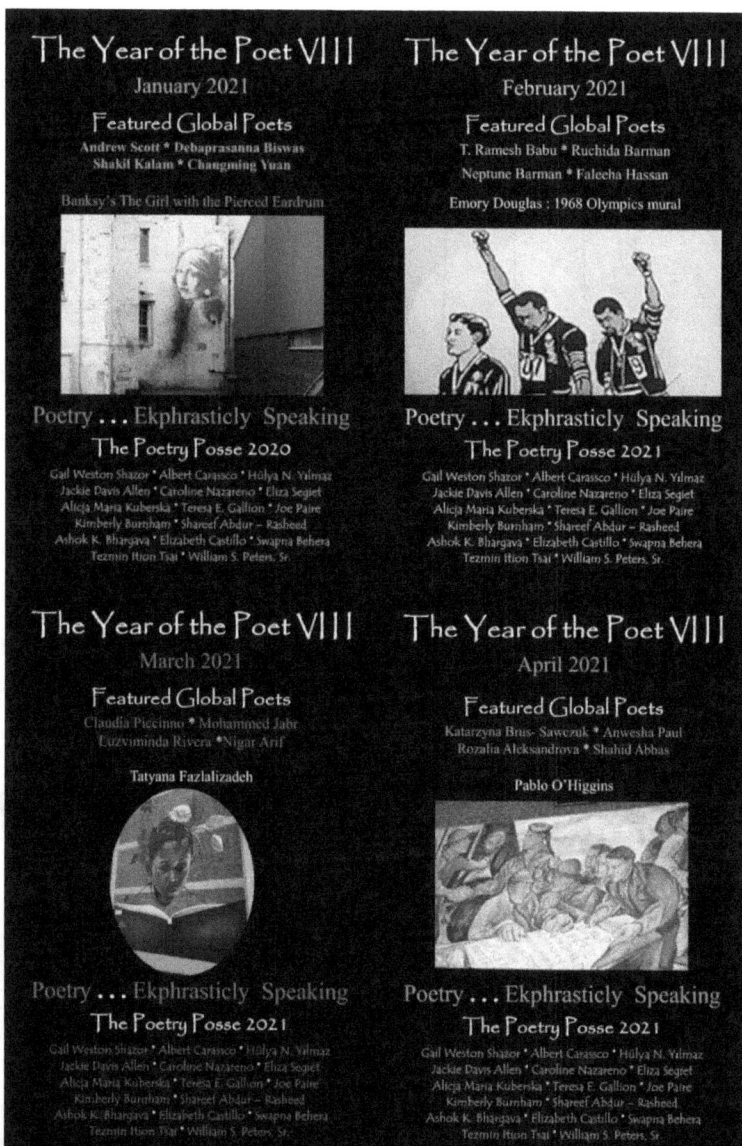

Now Available
www.innerchildpress.com/the-year-of-the-poet

Inner Child Press Anthologies

Now Available

www.innerchildpress.com/the-year-of-the-poet

Inner Child Press Anthologies

Now Available
www.innerchildpress.com/the-year-of-the-poet

Inner Child Press Anthologies

The Year of the Poet IX
January 2022

Featured Global Poets
Ratan Ghosh * Christine Neil-Wright
Andrew Scott * Ashok Kumar

Climate Change : The Ice Cap

Poetry . . . Ekphrasticly Speaking

The Poetry Posse 2021

Gail Weston Shazor * Albert Carasco * Hülya N. Yılmaz
Jackie Davis Allen * Caroline Nazareno * Eliza Segiet
Alicja Maria Kuberska * Teresa E. Gallion * Joe Paire
Kimberly Burnham * Shareef Abdur – Rasheed
Ashok K. Bhargava * Elizabeth Castillo * Swapna Behera
Tezmin Ition Tsai * William S. Peters, Sr.

The Year of the Poet IX
February 2022

Featured Global Poets
Roza Boyanova * Ramón de Jesús Núñez Duval
Mammad Ismayil * Tarana Turan Rahimli

Climate Change and Mountains

Poetry . . . Ekphrasticly Speaking

The Poetry Posse 2021

Gail Weston Shazor * Albert Carasco * Hülya N. Yılmaz
Jackie Davis Allen * Caroline Nazareno * Eliza Segiet
Alicja Maria Kuberska * Teresa E. Gallion * Joe Paire
Kimberly Burnham * Shareef Abdur – Rasheed
Ashok K. Bhargava * Elizabeth Castillo * Swapna Behera
Tezmin Ition Tsai * William S. Peters, Sr.

The Year of the Poet IX
March 2022

Featured Global Poets
Dimitris P. Kranjotis * Marlene Pasini
Kennedy Ochieng * Swayam Prashant

Climate Change and Space Debris

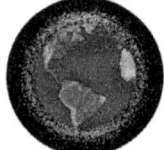

Poetry . . . Ekphrasticly Speaking

The Poetry Posse 2021

Gail Weston Shazor * Albert Carasco * Hülya N. Yılmaz
Jackie Davis Allen * Caroline Nazareno * Eliza Segiet
Alicja Maria Kuberska * Teresa E. Gallion * Joe Paire
Kimberly Burnham * Shareef Abdur – Rasheed
Ashok K. Bhargava * Elizabeth Castillo * Swapna Behera
Tezmin Ition Tsai * William S. Peters, Sr.

The Year of the Poet IX
April 2022

Featured Global Poets
Alonzo Gross * Dr. Debaprasanna Biswas
Monsif Beroual * Carol Aronoff

Climate Change and Oceans

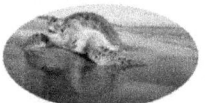

*Celebrating our 100th Edition *

Poetry . . . Ekphrasticly Speaking

The Poetry Posse 2021

Gail Weston Shazor * Albert Carasco * Hülya N. Yılmaz
Jackie Davis Allen * Caroline Nazareno * Eliza Segiet
Alicja Maria Kuberska * Teresa E. Gallion * Joe Paire
Kimberly Burnham * Shareef Abdur – Rasheed
Ashok K. Bhargava * Elizabeth Castillo * Swapna Behera
Tezmin Ition Tsai * William S. Peters, Sr.

Now Available
www.innerchildpress.com/the-year-of-the-poet

Inner Child Press Anthologies

The Year of the Poet IX
May 2022

Featured Global Poets
Ndaba Sibanda * Smrutiranjan Mohanty
Ajanta Paul * Monalisa Dash Dwibedy

Climate Change and Birds

Poetry . . . Ekphrasticly Speaking

The Poetry Posse 2021

Gail Weston Shazor * Albert Carasco * Hülya N. Yılmaz
Jackie Davis Allen * Caroline Nazareno * Eliza Segiet
Alicja Maria Kuberska * Teresa E. Gallion * Joe Paire
Kimberly Burnham * Shareef Abdur – Rasheed
Ashok K. Bhargava * Elizabeth Castillo * Swapna Behera
Tezmin Ition Tsai * William S. Peters, Sr.

The Year of the Poet IX
June 2022

Featured Global Poets
Yuan Changming * Azeezat Okunlola
Tanja Ajtić * Philip Chijioke Abonyi

Climate Change and Trees

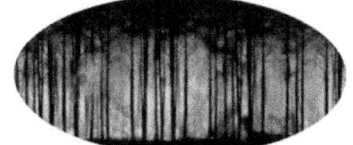

Poetry . . . Ekphrasticly Speaking

The Poetry Posse 2022

Gail Weston Shazor * Albert Carasco * Hülya N. Yılmaz
Jackie Davis Allen * Caroline Nazareno * Eliza Segiet
Alicja Maria Kuberska * Teresa E. Gallion * Joe Paire
Kimberly Burnham * Shareef Abdur – Rasheed
Ashok K. Bhargava * Elizabeth Castillo * Swapna Behera
Tezmin Ition Tsai * William S. Peters, Sr.

The Year of the Poet IX
July 2022

Featured Global Poets
**Michelle Joan Barulich * Mili Das
Anna Ferriero * Ujjal Mandal**

Climate Change and Animals

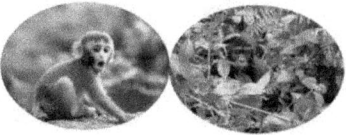

Poetry . . . Ekphrasticly Speaking

The Poetry Posse 2022

Gail Weston Shazor * Albert Carasco * Hülya N. Yılmaz
Jackie Davis Allen * Caroline Nazareno * Eliza Segiet
Alicja Maria Kuberska * Teresa E. Gallion * Joe Paire
Kimberly Burnham * Shareef Abdur – Rasheed
Ashok K. Bhargava * Elizabeth Castillo * Swapna Behera
Tezmin Ition Tsai * William S. Peters, Sr.

The Year of the Poet IX
August 2022

Featured Global Poets
**Pankhuri Sinha * Abdulloh Abdumominov
Caroline Turunç * Tali Cohen Shabtai**

Climate Change and Agriculture

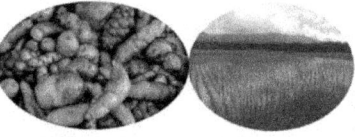

Poetry . . . Ekphrasticly Speaking

The Poetry Posse 2022

Gail Weston Shazor * Albert Carasco * Hülya N. Yılmaz
Jackie Davis Allen * Caroline Nazareno * Eliza Segiet
Alicja Maria Kuberska * Teresa E. Gallion * Joe Paire
Kimberly Burnham * Shareef Abdur – Rasheed
Ashok K. Bhargava * Elizabeth Castillo * Swapna Behera
Tezmin Ition Tsai * William S. Peters, Sr.

Now Available
www.innerchildpress.com/the-year-of-the-poet

Inner Child Press Anthologies

The Year of the Poet IX
September 2022

Featured Global Poets
Ngozi Olivia Osuoha * Biswajit Mishra
Sylwia K. Malinowska * Sajid Hussein

Climate Change and Wind and Weather Patterns

Poetry . . . Ekphrasticly Speaking

The Poetry Posse 2022

Gail Weston Shazor * Albert Carasco * Hülya N. Yılmaz
Jackie Davis Allen * Caroline Nazareno * Eliza Segiet
Alicja Maria Kuberska * Teresa E. Gallion * Joe Paire
Kimberly Burnham * Shareef Abdur – Rasheed
Ashok K. Bhargava * Elizabeth Castillo * Swapna Behera
Tezmin Ition Tsai * William S. Peters, Sr.

The Year of the Poet IX
October 2022

Featured Global Poets
Andrew Kouroupos * Brenda Mohammed
Carthornia Kouroupos * Faleeha Hassan

Climate Change and Oil and Power

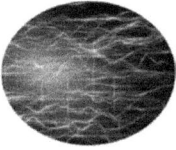 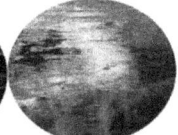

Poetry . . . Ekphrasticly Speaking

The Poetry Posse 2022

Gail Weston Shazor * Albert Carasco * Hülya N. Yılmaz
Jackie Davis Allen * Caroline Nazareno * Eliza Segiet
Alicja Maria Kuberska * Teresa E. Gallion * Joe Paire
Kimberly Burnham * Shareef Abdur – Rasheed
Ashok K. Bhargava * Elizabeth Castillo * Swapna Behera
Tezmin Ition Tsai * William S. Peters, Sr.

The Year of the Poet IX
November 2022

Featured Global Poets
Hema Ravi * Shafkat Aziz Hajam
Selma Kopic * Ibrahim Honjo

Climate Change : Time to Act

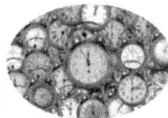 

Poetry . . . Ekphrasticly Speaking

The Poetry Posse 2022

Gail Weston Shazor * Albert Carasco * Hülya N. Yılmaz
Jackie Davis Allen * Caroline Nazareno * Eliza Segiet
Alicja Maria Kuberska * Teresa E. Gallion * Joe Paire
Kimberly Burnham * Shareef Abdur – Rasheed
Ashok K. Bhargava * Elizabeth Castillo * Swapna Behera
Tezmin Ition Tsai * William S. Peters, Sr.

The Year of the Poet IX
December 2022

Featured Global Poets
Elarbi Abdelfattah * Lorraine Cragg
Neha Bhandarkar * Robert Gibbons

Climate Change Bees, Butterflies and Insect Life

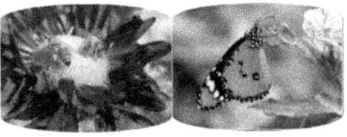

Poetry . . . Ekphrasticly Speaking

The Poetry Posse 2022

Gail Weston Shazor * Albert Carasco * Hülya N. Yılmaz
Jackie Davis Allen * Caroline Nazareno * Eliza Segiet
Alicja Maria Kuberska * Teresa E. Gallion * Joe Paire
Kimberly Burnham * Shareef Abdur – Rasheed
Ashok K. Bhargava * Elizabeth Castillo * Swapna Behera
Tezmin Ition Tsai * William S. Peters, Sr.

Now Available
www.innerchildpress.com/the-year-of-the-poet

Inner Child Press Anthologies

Now Available
www.innerchildpress.com/the-year-of-the-poet

Inner Child Press Anthologies

Now Available
www.innerchildpress.com/the-year-of-the-poet

Inner Child Press Anthologies

The Year of the Poet X
September 2023

Featured Global Poets
Eftichia Karpadeli * Chinh Nguyen
Nigar Agalarova * Carmela Cueva

Children : Difference Makers

~ Easton LaChappelle ~

The Poetry Posse 2023
Gail Weston Shazor * Albert Carasco * Hülya N. Yılmaz
Jackie Davis Allen * Caroline Nazareno * Kimberly Burnham
Alicja Maria Kuberska * Teresa E. Gallion * Joe Paire
Michelle Joan Barulich * Shareef Abdur – Rasheed
Ashok K. Bhargava * Elizabeth Castillo * Swapna Behera
Tezmin Ition Tsai * Eliza Segiet * William S. Peters, Sr.

The Year of the Poet X
October 2023

Featured Global Poets
CSP Shrivastava * Huniie Parker
Noreen Snyder * Ramkrishna Paul

Children : Difference Makers

~ Malala Yousafzai ~

The Poetry Posse 2023
Gail Weston Shazor * Albert Carasco * Hülya N. Yılmaz
Jackie Davis Allen * Caroline Nazareno * Kimberly Burnham
Alicja Maria Kuberska * Teresa E. Gallion * Joe Paire
Michelle Joan Barulich * Shareef Abdur – Rasheed
Ashok K. Bhargava * Elizabeth Castillo * Swapna Behera
Tezmin Ition Tsai * Eliza Segiet * William S. Peters, Sr.

The Year of the Poet X
November 2023

Featured Global Poets
Ibrahim Honjo * Balachandran Nair
Xanthi Hondrou-Hil * Francesco Favetta

Children : Difference Makers

~ Jean-Michel Basquiat ~

The Poetry Posse 2023
Gail Weston Shazor * Albert Carasco * Hülya N. Yılmaz
Jackie Davis Allen * Caroline Nazareno * Kimberly Burnham
Alicja Maria Kuberska * Teresa E. Gallion * Joe Paire
Michelle Joan Barulich * Shareef Abdur – Rasheed
Ashok K. Bhargava * Elizabeth Castillo * Swapna Behera
Tezmin Ition Tsai * Eliza Segiet * William S. Peters, Sr.

The Year of the Poet X
December 2023

Featured Global Poets
Caroline Laurent Turunc * Neha Bhandarkar
Shafkat Aziz Hajam * Elarbi Abdelfattah

Children : Difference Makers

~ Melati and Isabel Wijsen ~

The Poetry Posse 2023
Gail Weston Shazor * Albert Carasco * Hülya N. Yılmaz
Jackie Davis Allen * Caroline Nazareno * Kimberly Burnham
Alicja Maria Kuberska * Teresa E. Gallion * Joe Paire
Michelle Joan Barulich * Shareef Abdur – Rasheed
Ashok K. Bhargava * Elizabeth Castillo * Swapna Behera
Tezmin Ition Tsai * Eliza Segiet * William S. Peters, Sr.

Now Available
www.innerchildpress.com/the-year-of-the-poet

and there is much, much more !

visit . . .

www.innerchildpress.com/anthologies-sales-special.php

Also check out our Authors and all the wonderful Books Available at :

www.innerchildpress.com/authors-pages

World Healing World Peace 2020
Poets for Humanity

Now Available

www.worldhealingworldpeacepoetry.com

Now Available

www.worldhealingworldpeacepoetry.com

www.worldhealingworldpeacepoetry.com

World Healing World Peace
2012, 2014, 2016, 2018, 2020, 2022

Now Available

www.worldhealingworldpeacepoetry.com

Inner Child Press International

'building bridges of cultural understanding'

Meet the Board of Directors

William S. Peters, Sr.
Chair Person
Founder
Inner Child Enterprises
Inner Child Press

Hülya N Yılmaz
Director
Editing Services
Co-Chair Person

Fahredin B. Shehu
Director
Cultural Affairs

Elizabeth E. Castillo
Director
Recording Secretary

De'Andre Hawthorne
Director
Performance Poetry

Gail Weston Shazor
Director
Anthologies

Kimberly Burnham
Director
Cultural Ambassador
Pacific Northwest
USA

Ashok K. Bhargava
Director
WINAwards

Deborah Smart
Director
Publicity
Marketing

www.innerchildpress.com

Inner Child Press International
'building bridges of cultural understanding'

Meet our Cultural Ambassadors

Fahredin Shehu
Director of Cultural

Faleeha Hassan
Iraq ~ USA

Elizabeth E. Castillo
Philippines

Antoinette Coleman
Chicago
Midwest USA

Ananda Nepali
Nepal ~ Tibet
Northern India

Kimberly Burnham
Pacific Northwest
USA

Alicja Kuberska
Poland
Eastern Europe

Swapna Behera
India
Southeast Asia

Kolade O. Freedom
Nigeria
West Africa

Monsif Beroual
Morocco
Northern Africa

Ashok K. Bhargava
Canada

Tzemin Ition Tsai
Republic of China
Greater China

Alicia M. Ramirez
Mexico
Central America

Christena AV Williams
Jamaica
Caribbean

Louise Hudon
Eastern Canada

Aziz Mountassir
Morocco
Northern Africa

Shareef Abdur-Rasheed
Southeastern USA

Laure Charazac
France
Western Europe

Mohammad Ikbal Harb
Lebanon
Middle East

Mohamed Abdel
Aziz Shmeis
Egypt
Middle East

Hilary Mainga
Kenya
Eastern Africa

Josephus R. Johnson
Liberia

www.innerchildpress.com

This Anthological Publication
is underwritten solely by

Inner Child Press International

Inner Child Press is a Publishing Company Founded and Operated by Writers. Our personal publishing experiences provides us an intimate understanding of the sometimes daunting challenges Writers, New and Seasoned may face in the Business of Publishing and Marketing their Creative "Written Work".

For more Information

Inner Child Press International

www.innerchildpress.com

'building bridges of cultural understanding'

202 Wiltree Court, State College, Pennsylvania 16801

www.innerchildpress.com

~ fini ~

www.ingramcontent.com/pod-product-compliance
Lightning Source LLC
LaVergne TN
LVHW051042080426
835508LV00019B/1660